THE MAKING OF
OLIVER STONE'S

HEAVEN AND EARTH

"Heaven and Earth" screenplay based on

the autobiographical books by

Le Ly Hayslip

When Heaven and Earth Changed Places,

written with Jay Wurts,

published in hardcover by Doubleday, New York, and

in paperback by New American Library, New York;

AND

Child of War, Woman of Peace,

written with James Hayslip,

published in hardcover by Doubleday, New York

THE MAKING OF
OLIVER STONE'S

HEAVEN AND EARTH

Text by Michael Singer from the Screenplay by Oliver Stone

Introduction by Oliver Stone

with additional commentary by

Le Ly Hayslip and Hiep Thi Le

CHARLES E. TUTTLE COMPANY, INC.

BOSTON • RUTLAND, VERMONT • TOKYO

PUBLISHED BY CHARLES E. TUTTLE COMPANY, INC.

of Rutland, Vermont, and Tokyo, Japan

with editorial offices at 77 Central Street

Boston, Massachusetts 02109

Library of Congress Cataloging in Publication Data

Singer, Michael
    The making of Oliver Stone's Heaven and earth / text by Michael Singer from the screen-
play by Oliver Stone : based on the autobiographical books by Le Ly Hayslip, When Heaven
and earth changed places, written with Jay Wurts, and Child of war, woman of peace, written
with James Hayslip : introduction by Oliver Stone, with commentary by Le Ly Hayslip and
Hiep Thi Le.
        p.   cm.
    ISBN 0-8048-1991-2. -- ISBN 0-8048-1990-4 (pbk.)
    1. Heaven and earth (Motion picture)   I. Stone, Oliver   II. Hayslip, Le Ly
    III. Le, Hiep Thi   IV. Title
PN1997.H4123S56   1993   93-30123
                                                                             CIP

DESIGN BY SHERRY FATLA

First Edition

1 3 5 7 9 10 8 6 4 2

PRINTED IN HONG KONG BY MANDARIN OFFSET LTD.

CONTENTS

PART ONE

VIETNAM: THE REVERSE ANGLE

by Oliver Stone

America was in Vietnam for nearly fifteen years . . . but did we ever really see it? Even now, with more than 600,000 Vietnamese living in America as one of the latest waves of immigrants to flood into our country, these people remain a comfortable abstraction to most of their non-Asian neighbors.

Call it guilt, or just avoidance, but Americans still seem reluctant to deal with the simple, familiar humanity of the Vietnamese as a people. If we acknowledge their palpable flesh and blood—not to mention recognizable human emotions—how then can we, as a nation, cope with the memory of a war that reduced the Vietnamese to convenient stereotypes, making them all the more easy to kill with impunity? At best, they were to be pitied. At worst, they were to be slaughtered. And millions of them were.

Most American films made about the Vietnam War, including two of my own, have not featured prominent Vietnamese characters. *Platoon* and *Born on the Fourth of July* told specific, grunt's-eye-view stories of the hellish misery our foot soldiers went through in that far-off place.

What's been missing from the screen is the reverse angle on the Vietnamese: what the war—or wars—were like from the perspective of the people living in Vietnam, a country with more than a thousand rich years of history and culture. And more particularly, what were the experiences of the innocent peasant farmers, interested in little more than their seasonal plantings and harvestings, their families and kin, having enough to eat from month to month, praying to the Buddha and their ancestors? These hard-working souls, with one eye on the heaven above them and the other on the earth that brought forth sustenance and regenerative life, were the wars' most tragic victims.

Le Ly Hayslip was born to the Phung family in the Central Vietnamese village of Ky La. She was imbued with the beauty and strength of her culture by stern but loving and proud parents. During the course of surviving three wars, Le Ly was stripped of her innocence, her family ties, and a good measure of her dreams . . . for a time, anyway.

But finally—a true symbol of what's best in her country—Le Ly triumphed over every adversity. Hers is a spiritual odyssey, a journey into freedom, enlightenment, and social action.

This odyssey is at the heart of *Heaven and Earth*, and the reason I felt Le Ly's story deserved . . . no, demanded . . . to be told on film.

As an infantryman in Vietnam, I was distrustful of the Vietnamese—all Vietnamese—because they posed a threat to me and my friends. It wasn't until later that I recognized what the American GIs and Vietnamese civilians had in common: fear and the need to survive under any circumstance. We were suspicious of each other, but in fact we shared a common bond of cold sweat and jangled nerves.

All survivors are linked by this mutual agony. In his powerful books about the Holocaust, Nobel Peace Prize winner Elie Wiesel reminds us that survivors are all charged with a sacred mission: to serve as witnesses and teachers of what they suffered, thereby preventing such catastrophes from occurring again.

Perhaps that's why I keep returning to Vietnam, both actually and cinematically. Some have suggested that *Heaven and Earth* is the final third of my "Vietnam Trilogy." In fact, I could make twenty more films about the war, so great a role did it play in my life and the soul of our country and the world.

Le Ly has already told her own story in two powerful autobiographies—*When Heaven and Earth Changed Places* and *Child of War, Woman of Peace*—both of which served as the foundation for *Heaven and Earth*. But Le Ly has gone several steps further. With limitless commitment and passion, she has literally brought it all back home with her East Meets West Foundation and the medical institutions maintained by the organization in Central Vietnam. It's one thing to write about your tragedies. It's quite another to transform them into positive action, to light that proverbial candle rather than curse the darkness. It has been a great honor and privilege to have had some small connection with Le Ly's organization, and to see with my own eyes the results of its humanitarian actions.

Among other shared experiences on opposite ends of the globe, Le Ly and I both had to tolerate any number of lies from soldiers and politicians in our respective countries. Their final goal, of course, was to put guns in our hands and ask us to point them at each other. Le Ly was abused by soldiers of both the North and South. I was born in 1946, in New York City, at the dawn of the Cold War. My father raised me as a Republican and instilled in me a fear of the Russians and communism. By the standards of the fifties, he was right, but he never expected—

4

and was horrified—when his son went to war to fight for the beliefs he had been raised with.

I arrived in Saigon in June of 1965 as a teacher, nineteen-years-old and gung-ho for the cause. The Marines and the Army First Infantry troops were drinking in Tu Do Street, brandishing weapons and firing them into the air in the first blush of our victory. We were the good guys, we were going to win. It was the war of my generation. It was glorious.

When I returned to Vietnam in 1967 as an infantryman, the first thing that struck me was that it had all changed for the worse. The Vietnamese who welcomed us in 1965 had now started the slow process of taking our dollars and hating us for it. Corruption and prostitution were rampant. PX supplies were being ripped off by South Vietnamese and American lifer sergeants (who were later implicated in scandals). Many people went home in body bags, while others made millions of dollars. For every combatant there were six or seven noncombatants, many of whom ate steak and lobster dinners each night in Da Nang or Cam Ranh or Saigon or Qui Nhon or Quang Tri or Bien-hoa.

To the boonie rats and grunts, the situation in the rear began to resemble Las Vegas or Miami Beach in all their worst aspects. We brought a corporate mentality to Vietnam. When Lyndon Johnson pulled out of the presidential race in March, 1968, it was metaphorically over. The grunts sensed it right away; we were never going to win, but we had to withdraw with a semblance of dignity.

That semblance of dignity took four more years of deceit and death, and in the moral vacuum, there was never any clear reason to us why we should die. To the Vietnamese, the rationale was simpler: it was their land, and they were defending it from foreign invaders. But with us, dissension and mutiny grew in the ranks between draftees and their sergeants and officers. Fraggings occurred on a scale never seen in modern war; black/white relations grew worse in the wake of Martin Luther King's assassination. Marijuana and, eventually, heroin usage engulfed a portion of the troops. The ultimate corruption was, of course, sending only the poor and uneducated to the war—in fact, practicing class warfare wherein the middle and upper classes could avoid the war by going to college or paying a psychiatrist.

I am sure to this day that if the sons of the middle and upper classes had gone to Vietnam, their mothers and fathers would have ended the war a hell of a lot sooner; in fact, politicians' children, if not politicians themselves, should be sent to every war first. Instead, the working class was sent, and these GIs, already so full of anger and frustration at their own society, turned their rage against the "enemy." And if they demonstrated a profound lack of respect and compassion for the people of Vietnam, it was clearly a response to the lack of respect and compassion that was demonstrated toward them back in the United States. And when they got home, it was even worse: heroes without portfolio, and all too often, without arms or legs or sight or sexuality.

I am also sure to this day that we were destined to lose this war before we ever fought it. Every war is won before it is ever fought; I am paraphrasing the great Chinese military strategist Sun-tzu. We were destined to lose because this war had no moral purpose and was fought without any moral integrity. And we did lose because basically, as a character in *Platoon* says, "We were not the good guys anymore."

The point of *Heaven and Earth* is neither to vilify the Americans and glorify the Vietnamese nor to create new "politically correct" stereotypes to replace the old ones. Good and bad people of all backgrounds and persuasions blew through Le Ly's life, and of course she finally did succeed in the United States, as did millions of immigrants before her. She's now the daughter of two countries, two cultures; and her three sons also share the merged heritage.

Buddhist spirituality, reverence for ancestors, and respect for the land were three of the strongest elements of Le Ly's story that attracted my interest. None of these themes had yet been approached in a film about Vietnam, and I was eager to explore them dramatically and visually.

I also wanted *Heaven and Earth* to respond to, in part, the blind militarism and mindless revisionism of the Vietnam War as typified by a certain odious brand of thinking that has snaked its way into our culture over the past decade or so, in which the conflict is refought in comic-book style by American superheroes, with a brand new ending . . . we win! Within the moronic context of these ideas, hundreds of nameless, faceless, Vietnamese are blithely and casually shot, stabbed, and blown to smithereens, utterly without the benefit of human consideration. Entire villages are triumphantly laid to waste, with not one microsecond of thought or care given to those inside the little bamboo hamlets being napalmed. Who were they?

There were names and faces and histories attached to those bodies littering one end of Vietnam to the other between 1963 and 1975. *Heaven and Earth* is the story of just one family, and as Le Ly constantly and generously reminds me, many others suffered even more than the Phungs.

Le Ly Hayslip and Vietnam have known too much darkness, too many deferred dreams. And Le Ly truly is a woman of Vietnam: beautiful, ferocious, soulful, stubborn, emotional, musical, and, yes, sometimes frustrating and even infuriating. But like her country, she denies defeat. And in the end, there's the lingering power of love.

It's the love the women of Vietnam needed to hold their crumbling families together, to bury their dead husbands and sons, to tend family members who returned home maimed in body or in spirit, to keep Vietnamese culture alive and thriving in the many *Viet Kieu* immigrant communities that now exist throughout the United States and the world. And it's the love that sustains the aptly-named Mother's Love Clinic in Le Ly's own village of Ky La, the Peace Village Medical

6

Center at China Beach in Da Nang, and the recently opened Village of Hope home for displaced children in Thanh Khe—all supported by the East Meets West Foundation.

During the long and arduous filming of *Heaven and Earth* in Thailand, Vietnam, and the United States, Le Ly was a godsend, working by my side every day, not just as a creative and technical consultant, but also as a spiritual collaborator. I had to learn her way of life from the ground up; it was like learning to swim. She was very patient, very thoughtful, a good teacher.

As for me, I was trying to push Le Ly to deal honestly with her memory, just as I did in my own case when I made *Platoon*. What do you actually remember? And Le Ly had many significant flashbacks, dramatic moments, and personal traumas in dealing with her past. She would often break down while watching us re-create some of the more harrowing moments of her life. On the brighter side, she fell in love with our reconstructed version of Ky La, her home village, and often slept in "her" house, cooking dinner and taking care of the dogs, pigs, and chickens. She relived her life through her work on the film, with all of its joys and nightmares, hopes and regrets. The film benefited immeasurably from her daily presence.

With *Heaven and Earth*, we hope to bring Le Ly's message—and Le Ly's Vietnam—to moviegoers around the world. There are so many wounds yet to be healed, not just between Vietnamese and Americans, but also between the people of a divided Vietnamese community as well. We had Vietnamese and *Viet Kieu* of wildly different political sympathies working together on the film, and their divisions were quickly swept aside in their shared quest to reveal the light that emanates from their culture, their ways, their history, and their home.

Le Ly has declared that her mission is to heal the hearts and minds of all those willing to listen to her "song of enlightenment," a song that transcends the transparent and petty barriers of politics, ideologies, religion, and prejudice. It is, she reminds us, a song that our hearts have been singing since the moment of our birth.

It is this song of peace, rather than war and vengeance, that deserves to be passed down from one generation to the next. Le Ly and I both lived to tell the tale. Let's hope that our children don't have to tell the same one.

The war has been over for almost twenty years. Isn't it time, at last, to begin the peace?

THE STORY

Adapted by Michael Singer
from the screenplay by Oliver Stone

Before the wars, there was always the land.

And to the farmers of Vietnam, the land was all that mattered. The wheel of life turned resolutely forward, the timeless cycles of planting and harvesting defining the villagers' existence.

Before the wars, all the gods were firmly in place. Father Heaven, Ong Troi, *was the keeper of all human fate, the master of unseen powers and mysteries. Mother Earth,* Me Dat, *provided food and water for the wells and fields. And between* Troi va Dat—*Heaven and Earth—were the people, striving to follow the Lord Buddha's teachings by walking the middle path and keeping all opposing forces in balance . . .*

VIETNAM

It is the early 1950s in Ky La, a rice-farming village in Central Vietnam, under the domination of France for nearly seventy years as part of its vast Indochinese colonial empire. But the French rulers are far away in Saigon, Hanoi, or Paris. In Ky La, life goes on as it has for a thousand years.

The villagers harvest the rice, with cuts on their hands and leeches on their legs. Farmers thresh the rice with wooden flails. Children ride water buffalo like pets. A little girl chases ducks with a stick along a narrow, unpaved path. Grizzled grandmothers carry buckets of gravel on shoulder poles, like oxen laboring in a yoke.

Enjoying this idyllic beauty is a young child, Le Ly, of the Phung family. And the bucolic peace of Ky La gives no indication that she is about to be propelled on an odyssey which will take her through nearly four decades of turbulence, despair, enlightenment, and triumph.

This is Le Ly's story . . . Vietnam's story: what happened to a woman, a people, and a nation when Heaven and Earth changed places.

that has borne silent witness to hundreds of years of history and tradition. A soft wind, perfumed with the sweet, pungent smells of Ky La, blows through the fields, swaying the rice plants.

Papa and Le Ly survey their village, admiring the towering limestone peaks that overhang it like protective sentinels. "Bay Ly, you see all this? You understand that a country is more than just dirt, rivers, and forests?"

"Yes," his daughter says respectfully.

"You know Sau may not come back? I told you many times the Chinese ruled our land. Many died. Le Loi, the Trung sisters, and your ancestor Phung Thi Chinh fought to throw out the Chinese. Your grandfather fought and died against the Japanese before you were born. We suffered much . . . . When the Japanese came, your mother and I were taken to Da Nang to build a runway for their airplanes. We worked like slaves. Our reward was a bowl of rice and another day of life.

"Freedom is never a gift, Bay Ly. It must be won and won again. You know that?"

"I do," answers Le Ly, attempting to understand.

"Good."

Papa points to the verdant landscape.

"This land—Vietnam—is now yours too. If the enemy comes back, you must be both a daughter and a son now."

And putting his arm around his daughter's shoulders, Papa walks Le Ly through the fields toward their village.

But Ky La is caught in the wash of historical tides that take little pity on the lives of simple rice farmers. And when the village dogs begin barking at a distant thunder, Le Ly, tending a water buffalo, is

snapped out of a midday reverie by a vision even more dreamlike: descending from the glaring light of the Vietnam sun is a giant, dull green, monstrous bird. The buffalo grunts, scared, and trots toward the trees. A great wind whips Le Ly's clothes, and sends her farmer's hat, the ubiquitous lampshade-shaped *non la*, sailing across the fields. The ankle-deep water is rippling beneath the downblast.

Le Ly, never having seen such a sight, thinks she is about to die.

She falls to her knees, holding fast to the earth, peeking up to see a giant stepping out of the monster bird and onto the marshy ground of Ky La.

He is a splendid-looking man—an American, crisply clean in starched fatigues with a yellow scarf tucked into his shirt and a golden patch on his shoulder. His black boots, bloused with battle pants, shine like beetle shells. The American's hands raise binoculars to his eyes, scanning the tree line around Ky La, ignoring Le Ly. Turning toward the village, she sees South Vietnamese Republican troops coming up the road in formation, with jeeps, a tank, armored carriers, and American advisory personnel. It's the new order of things. Papa runs out, grabbing Le Ly and carrying her off to safety.

Ky La is now under the control of Republican troops and their American cohorts. "Your village will be safe," a mustached Republican colonel tells the people. "Many of you will be asked to take militia training, so you will be prepared to resist the Communist rebels. You will receive food and some money if you help. Your children will be sent to camps for military training."

Ky La is transformed into a military fortress. Barbed wire is strung up by the Republican soldiers. A bright sign announcing the village's new name—Thon Binh Ky—is mounted on cement girders in red and yellow, the colors of the Republican flag. Indeed, the Republican flag itself is flown high above the village from the common ground.

The Republicans build a watchtower, complete with 50-caliber machine-gun mounts. An American Green Beret adviser oversees the construction of barbed-wire barricades.

"What are they? Americans?" Le Ly asks her twenty-year-old sister, Kim.

"They say they all have blind blue eyes behind the glasses," Kim replies. "If you take their shoes off, they have soft feet and cry in pain. Take their glasses and their boots and they can't fight."

Inside the new schoolroom, Le Ly and the other children learn the Republican way from their schoolteacher, Manh, who is in the monetary service of the South.

"What will you do if you see a Viet Cong, or hear about someone who's helping them?" he asks the class.

"Turn him in to the soldiers!" they enthusiastically respond in unison.

"Good. And get a big reward for every Viet Cong you help capture."

True to their changing environment, the children of the village now play war games on the high ground rather than fly kites. Some kids want to play Republican soldiers. Others want to be Viet Cong. Battle lines are being drawn throughout the entire village, from young to old.

One night, the Viet Cong return to Ky La, dragging school-teacher Manh out of his house and forcing him to his knees. Le Ly watches with her parents from across the lotus pond as Manh is cut down with two short rifle bursts.

The Republican flag comes down. The Viet Cong flag now flies over the village. "Anyone who touches that flag will get the same as that traitor," promises the young VC captain who previously took Sau and Bon off to war.

The Viet Cong rip down the Republican constructions and toss the debris into a giant bonfire on the common ground. "We will teach you how to operate radios, build mines and traps, run hospitals, move supplies without touching a road," promises the captain to the vil-

lagers. "Ky La is our village now. We have given it back to you. . . .
We are the soldiers of liberation. Help us win and you will keep your
property and everything else you love."

Mama asks the captain if there is any news of her two sons.

"North, they're training in the North," he responds brusquely. "There is no time now for sons and mothers."

The Viet Cong wonder why Le Ly isn't out with the youth brigade. Papa tells them that he needs her on the farm. "For all the help she is around here!" answers Mama disapprovingly over a family dinner. "Maybe we should send her away with Sau. That would teach her the value of a good day's work."

"Do not talk like that!" Papa responds angrily."

"Bay Ly must do her work like everyone else," Mama continues. "She thinks she's one little princess—too good for work, too busy blinking her eyes at good-for-nothing schoolboys—"

"That's not true, Mama," Le Ly speaks up in her own defense. "The big boys bother me all the time now."

"You be quiet, little princess! A woman doesn't talk like that!" Mama hits Le Ly on the forehead, and in a flash, Papa grabs his wife's wrist.

"Don't hit her again, do you hear me! Do you want to send all your children to Hanoi or Saigon? Are you in such a hurry to get rid of your family? Maybe you're tired of your husband too! Maybe I should go in the army!"

"I *do* want my babies back," Mama cries.

"What kind of woman are you! Did my mother not teach you anything about family? Family is everything! All I want is my family. If I can't have my family around me, what's the point of living any longer?"

"Why are you so selfish?" Mama shouts back. "The French, the Japanese, and now the Americans are trampling on us. It's better they go north now and fight for the right thing. We have a choice. War is coming, you stupid, selfish man!"

Papa, frustrated, slaps his wife across the cheek. She runs from the room, Le Ly following. "Forgive him, Mama," Le Ly pleads with her mother. "He's so angry. Don't cry."

Suddenly, Mama toughens and turns on her daughter. "I made

your Papa lose face in front of everyone. If you ever do that to a husband, I'll have both your cheeks hurting—one from him and one from me."

One night, Le Ly dreams of Sau; he has been captured, blindfolded, and beaten, and has bruises along his nose and legs. He is lying on a helicopter floor, terrified. Americans in the chopper scream at Sau and two other Viet Cong prisoners. "Hey, buddy! . . . This is it. You talk. Now. Or 'Bye, Charlie'—you dig, asshole?"

Sau shakes his head, scared but defiant.

"All right . . . it's your ass . . . kiss it good-bye!" And the American lifts Sau, who is now dangling at the door, looking down at Vietnamese earth. He falls. No yell, no scream. A small death to the American crewman who gazes numbly as he watches the descent of Sau.

Le Ly starts awake from her dream in cold terror, feeling the death of her brother.

The village's wizard, a strange-looking, eccentric man, makes his way to the Phung house. Mama shows the wizard her two sons' dried navel cords in a box. "The older one, Bon, is strong and healthy," the gray-bearded mystic tells her. "The younger one, Sau, is in a place too gray for me to see."

"No, no, that is not true!" Mama cries. "I know he's alive. I feel it in my womb. God would not do this. We have hurt no one."

"You hear funny noises? Maybe voices—last night in the rain?" he asks.

"I did," Le Ly responds, remembering her dream.

"Well, here's your problem then. Your spirit house is too small. You have a relative who needs some shelter, that's all. Just build a little shrine outside and things will be fine."

Without another word, the wizard leaves. Le Ly weeps. the world as she knows it is now starting to come apart.

Time passes. Le Ly, no longer playing at war, has now been absorbed into it as part of the Viet Cong cadre. A Republican patrol is ambushed on a village road; booby traps that Le Ly helped to build now explode. A small battle erupts; shouts of scared, dying men. The Republicans with their American allies return and rocket the village from hovering helicopters as reinforcements rush in under fire. One young Viet Cong girl releases a grenade that kills her, a comrade, and two Republican soldiers.

The dead VC girls are praised by their captain in the cave hide-out. They lie in coffins next to other wooden boxes, that are empty, and waiting for additional martyrs. The captain calls them "heroines who will live forever on our blackboard of honor . . . . Only in battle or by your own hands will you be immortalized." Le Ly listens, deeply moved.

In the morning fog a few days later, Le Ly is on early sentry duty along the road leading into the village. The mist envelops all, as Le Ly almost drifts off to sleep. Suddenly the fog lifts and she is startled by a teeming mass of Republican soldiers coming up the road. Panicked, she jumps up, the troops already past her, close to the village. She walks nonchalantly along the road, spotted in passing by the lethal-looking Vietnamese Ranger forces with their bright yellow scarves. As the last of this group passes her, Le Ly peels off her top two shirts—the first a red, the second white. The remaining shirt, a black one, signals danger all around.

Another Viet Cong scout spots Le Ly in the black shirt and scuttles in the opposite direction to warn her comrades. But a sharp-eyed Republican scout sees her, chases. Gunfire is heard . . .

Republican troops scour the village in search of Le Ly. Helped by a collaborator, they find her. The Rangers haul Le Ly away from her family home over the cries and protests of her parents.

Now she is in the hands of the enemy, in the notorious My Thi Prison, an interrogator waiting with a full range of medieval-looking torture implements. Off to the side is an American, with no badges or identifying unit marks.

"Tell me quickly. Why were you on the road?" demands Le Ly's interrogator.

"I was picking berries—"

But the interrogator cuts her off with a screamed "Liar!" and a blow across the face. The interrogator escalates his attacks. Le Ly is kicked, beaten, accused of being a VC cadre girl. A wire is clipped to each of her thumbs; her wrists are strapped down. With each denial, Le Ly receives a jolt of electricity. The interrogator, waving a scalpel, warns Le Ly that if she doesn't begin talking, she will receive even worse punishment.

After spending a horrible night manacled to thirty other prisoners, all with similar badges of abuse seared into their faces and bodies, Le Ly is brought to a courtyard with two other young girls.

They are tied to a post, and sweet, sticky honey is slathered across their feet and ankles. There are anthills all around the post, and soon the huge, black insects are stinging the three girls' legs and feet.

Morning grinds slowly into afternoon, the girls squirming in exhausted pain, their legs swollen purple with ant bites.

A soldier squats next to a bucket, rolls up his sleeves, and pulls out a glistening water snake about half the length of his arm.

He drops it into Le Ly's shirt, then does the same, with two more serpents, to the other girls.

The guards enjoy the girls' agonies. Le Ly reaching the outer limits of suffering, now redoubles her inner strength, screaming at the guards, at the sky . . . a warrior.

And soon the young warrior, bloodied, brutalized, but unbowed, is released to her family, who have paid a large bribe to insure her freedom. As Le Ly enters Ky La, Papa angrily leads his daughter through their village, now filled with suspicious faces. Neighbors avoid Le Ly's glances. Nobody gets out of My Thi so quickly, they think, even for a bribe.

The Viet Cong, believing Le Ly talked in exchange for her freedom, send the young soldiers Loi and Mau to snatch her from her parents' grasp, just as the Republicans did before them.

In an overgrown forest, wet with rain and humidity, Loi—the young Viet Cong who courted Le Ly at the dance in the caves—roughly pushes her to a small, makeshift "court-martial."

"Our men were betrayed; how else could the Americans know so much?" barks a woman cadre leader. "The village is filled with traitors . . . so I ask you, what should we do with these people? We must give these people a lesson they will never forget."

Loi and Mau yank Le Ly out of the meeting and deeper into the jungle. They come to a swampy ground and a small clearing. In the midst of it is a large hole in the earth.

Loi forces Le Ly to her knees and presses her face out over the yawning hole. It is to be her grave. Le Ly pleads her innocence. "What kind of deal did you make to get out of My Thi?" shouts Loi.

"My mother bribed an official. Why don't you believe me?"

Loi presses his rifle barrel to Le Ly's temple. Reconciled with the inevitable, she awaits the bullet that will take away her life, memories, future.

But suddenly Loi is on top of Le Ly, raping her, brutally taking both her innocence and pride.

"What happens next is up to you," Loi tells her. "If you talk we'll kill your whole family. Get the hell out of here!"

It is 1966. Ky La is no longer Le Ly's haven, no longer her safe place of childhood and nurturing. She and Mama travel to the anonymous maelstrom of Saigon, the teeming, corrupt capital of the South. Exhausted from days of travel, their clothes dirty, Mama and Le Ly enter a bustling market. Before their eyes a Buddhist monk is arrested by the white-uniformed Saigon police. Le Ly is shocked to see a man of God treated so roughly by the authorities.

But good fortune beckons. Mama and Le Ly find themselves in the splendor of a French Colonial mansion, applying for domestic positions in this home of the aristocratic Anh and his regal but ill wife, Madame Lien. Le Ly is immediately bewitched by Anh . . . his soft features, high cheekbones, wispy beard, and kind disposition.

As time passes, there are small exchanges between Anh and Le Ly: a glance, a slight stroking of her hair. She melts beneath his gaze. One night he caresses Le Ly, pulls her close, then retreats. Never has she been treated so gently by anyone. Life suddenly has a purpose, a

"Do you think a girl like you means anything to him? And now you're going to have his bastard. Well, you'll just have to get rid of it."

Mama tries to abort Le Ly's baby by feeding her daughter herbs and making her jump down the stairs. But the girl is strong, and so is the child inside her.

The child grows. One day, Le Ly, six months pregnant, whispers a hurried prayer of expiation at Anh's family shrine, in front of the old family portraits.

"What are you doing Le Ly?" inquires the coldly elegant Madame Lien.

"I'm expecting a child," says Le Ly timidly.

"Yes, I know. We learned it from the herbalist. Who is the father?"

"A boy. Someone I met in the park. You don't know him."

"And why are you burning incense?" continues Madame Lien in her pointed interrogation.

"Because I don't want the baby. I was praying to be forgiven."

"In front of my husband's ancestors?"

Madame Lien grows bolder in her assertions. "Well, Le Ly, I have another explanation. I believe the father of your baby is my husband. . . . You know I am not well, Le Ly. But I have given my husband sons as fine as any woman could have given him. Don't think you won't pay for what you've done."

Madame Lien orders Mama and Le Ly out of the house. Mama, terrified at being thrown back into the streets of Saigon, pleads:

"But Le Ly is no threat to you! She has nothing for a proper man. She's just a country girl—an ignorant, foolish, stupid child—a maid who'll never be a bride. She's nothing. Worthless!"

"Absolutely not!" replies Madame Lien. "I won't have her in my house. Not as a nanny, not as a housekeeper."

Anh has heard everything. His eyes are gentle but distant from Le Ly.

"I won't throw you into the street," he tells Mama. "But I can't ask my wife to let you live with us."

Anh will send them back to Da Nang in Central Vietnam and send money every month until the baby is born.

Le Ly is heartbroken by this rejection by the first man she has every truly loved. . . .

Two months later, a hardened Le Ly is selling bootlegged items to American infantrymen in the crowded streets of Da Nang. The city resembles a border boomtown, chockablock with soldiers, peasants, merchants, hookers, psychedelic bars, and noodle stalls. She is now eight months pregnant, and has learned Pidgin English to communicate with her GI targets.

"Hey, GI, number one cigarette here, very cheap . . . you look. And chocolate . . . white chocolate, one hundred piaster, you buy smokes, you want bottle Johnnie Walker, I give you. Four hundred piaster. . . ."

A blond, curly-haired GI leaps off a truck. "Hey, how about some boom boom, baby," he fliply asks Le Ly. "Give you ten bucks right now!"

"Me no hooker," she answers with some anger. "You go bar, cheap Charlie. Find plenty girl boom you."

"No you, little big mouth. Come on! Fifteen bucks. Watcha hiding?" He taps her swollen belly. "Fifty bucks!"

"You *dinky dau* GI. Fuck off . . . "

Soon after this exchange, Le Ly is confronted by some of the "White Mice," Da Nang's less-than-honest policemen. Searching her goods, they find a bag of marijuana. Then the cops wait for their payoff, and Le Ly retains her freedom.

The war has affected all members of the Phung family. Le Ly is living with her sister Kim, now a Da Nang bargirl. Kim is almost unrecognizable from her plainer days in Ky La—beehive hairdo, rouge, false eyelashes, polished fingernails, high heels, and lipstick that obscures her unsightly harelip.

One day, there's a bang at the door of Kim's cheap, crowded, garish little apartment. Le Ly opens it to see Paul, one of her sister's

GI boyfriends. He's just in from the field—rifle in hand, death in his eyes.

"Where's Kim?" he asks brusquely, pushing his way inside. "I'll wait for her, little sister. Get me a beer," Paul orders Le Ly, who wearily goes to the rear of the apartment to find one.

There is another knock at the door. The GI flings it open, expecting Kim—but instead finds Papa, who now looks much older. "I look for Kim," he tells Paul in broken English. "Me daughter. Kim here?"

Le Ly, stricken by the voice of a father she has not seen for a year, immediately hides.

"Kim gone for hours. No. Go away. No buy," Paul tells Papa, not understanding the old man's English.

"Please. Me Papa. No see long time," Papa says insistently.

"Papa san, *didi mau*, get lost. Stupid gook asshole."

Le Ly, peeking through the curtain, watches Paul push her father out the door, slamming it in the old man's face.

Kim enters her tacky apartment with Papa in tow. Le Ly, watching secretly, sees Paul kissing Kim in front of her embarrassed Papa. "Baby, been too long, six weeks in the bush. I need it bad. Now, babe, now—"

"Paul, not good time. My father come long way to see me—"

"He's got time. I don't. Get him out of here."

"Papa," says Kim, contritely but firmly. "Paul is my man. He pays the bills. Give me a little time. You come back in two hours." And with this modest apology, she heads into the bedroom with Paul.

Le Ly is aching to go to her father, but looks with shame at her pregnant stomach.

Later, Paul exits the apartment, satiated for the moment.

"I came to see your sister," Papa stiffly tells Kim when he returns.

"Oh, she's out at work. Selling near the base."

"Is she doing well?" Papa asks.

"Oh, she's lazy, but I help her all I can."

"And the baby?"

"I don't know why she had to go and seduce her master's husband."

Le Ly is devastated to hear this coming from her sister.

"Yes, she has brought shame on us," says Papa sadly. "An unwed mother." Glaring at Kim, he adds, "But she is not the only one who has brought shame to us."

"I do the best I can, Papa," Kim says in her own defense. "I'm going to be late for work."

Papa nods, distracted, a lonely old stick of a man. Unknowingly, he is inches from Le Ly.

"Kim, when you see Bay Ly, tell her I came to see her. Tell her I miss her very much and she shouldn't worry about being punished for her mistake. Life finds a way to balance itself . . . will you tell her that for me?"

"Of course, Papa. And me?"

"And you too, my little one . . ." And with those words of compassion and forgiveness, the old man leaves.

Le Ly, in tears, steps into view of Kim. "Your boyfriend treated Papa so bad! This is not the way Papa taught us to be."

"Do you think I like what I'm doing?" responds an angered Kim. "Somebody has to make a living; you sure don't help. I don't know why I listen to Mama and let you stay! My boyfriends all complain about you. Too many people in one room! Pregnant woman are bad luck!"

"How disrespectful you are!" Le Ly admonishes Kim. "If Papa—A foreigner! An invader! You sleep with the enemy! You betray your family!"

Kim has had enough. "I'll marry one too and get the hell out of this goddamn country! And as for you, you've worn out your welcome here. No more charity for you! Get out—right now! Get out! Do you think you're the only one Papa loves! You're spoiled, spoiled!"

Le Ly finds herself out in the street with her few meager belongings. A GI truck makes a brief stop near her and throws out some garbage. Le Ly searches through the trash for food and other discarded items of value.

She comes to a dead stop, terrified. In the trash is the dismembered body of a young prostitute in a transparent plastic bag. Le Ly recoils in horror and disgust. Life has been desecrated all over her country, losing its value and purpose. The traditions are dying by the moment.

But new life will find a way, and Le Ly soon gives birth to a healthy baby boy in a crowded birthing clinic. Le Ly names her child Hung.

Months pass, and Le Ly struggles to raise Hung amid the increasing proliferation of prostitutes, slavers, pimps, black-marketeers.

In the officious environs of the US Army Employment Office, Le Ly applies for a job with Hung in tow. She is interviewed by a young sergeant, whose outwardly friendly appearance belies something more unsavory just beneath the surface.

"The Korean club is looking for a hostess in their bar," he cheerfully informs Le Ly. "Good hours, mostly daytime, great money. Home early. Koreans don't hanky panky like Americans do . . . good for your babysan.

"And," he continues, now squeezing Le Ly's hand, "I will have no problem placing you there, provided of course . . . you play ball. You understand that American expression: play ball?

"What I mean, Le Ly, is the old army game . . . you scratch my back and I scratch yours. You're a big girl. I think you know what that means."

Unfortunately for Le Ly, she understands only too well. "Please, mister, open this door right now! Right now or I yell. I no siclo girl."

"Go ahead, scream your head off," the sergeant threatens, blocking her way. "No one's around."

Le Ly, infuriated by this latest assault on her dignity, pulls up a metal chair, swings it full force into the frosted glass of the door, and shatters it with a loud crash. She orders some workers to call the Military Police.

Le Ly is astonished that the MPs actually arrive and take the young sergeant away in handcuffs. It is one of her first victories. And she admires the fact that Americans arrested one of their own.

Soon Le Ly is back on the streets hawking her black-market goods. One of her targets is a big naval base surrounded by signs of decay, prostitution, and corruption. Big Mike, an MP sergeant, greets Le Ly. "Hey, you look beaucoup sad."

"Hi, Big Mike, no good day," she says.

"Well, I got something might change your mood. See those grunts over there?" he says, pointing at two clean-faced young Marines in fresh fatigues. "They're short-timers, leaving for the world today. They want a real souvenir. They want boom boom you."

"Beaucoup boom boom there," says Le Ly, pointing to the ramshackle hooker bars just outside of the base's perimeter.

Big Mike pleads. "Look, Le Ly, these pencil dicks are clean, they been in the bush since they got here. They're willing to pay twenty bucks each head."

"Le Ly good girl," she emphasizes again, tired of resisting. "Fuck off, Big Mike."

Big Mike pulls a wad of bills from his breast pocket. He offers Le Ly two hundred dollars. Her eyes widen at the sight of so much cash. Forcing herself, she says, "No deal, Big Mike. Le Ly not that kind of girl."

Big Mike ups the ante. Four hundred dollars, with fifty going to him for commission. "Support your family for a year easy! What's so bad about it? Fifteen minutes, it ain't even work. What are they gonna do that ain't been done already? . . . Come on, send the poor bastards home with a smile."

He sticks the roll of green cash in Le Ly's hand. There is Hung, now one and a half years old, to think about. There's her parents. Three hundred and fifty dollars can buy so much in wartime Vietnam. . . . And so, she allows herself to be bought.

Having received news that her parents are sick, Le Ly returns to Ky La. Or what used to be Ky La. Now it is all but unrecognizable, devastated, dominated by a huge American military base with its roaring helicopters and crashing artillery. There is a shantytown on the main road leading into the village, populated by the refuse of war, the crippled, the maimed. Homes are caved in. There are packs of stray dogs. An American plane sprays the fields with a venomous cloud of pesticide.

Le Ly sees a wretched old woman sitting beneath a tree. It is Mama. She's distracted, red betel juice running from her mouth like a vampire.

"Bay Ly, what are you doing here?" she asks her frightened daughter.

"I heard there was trouble. Where is Papa?"

Mama tells Le Ly a story of how Papa was humiliated, beaten, and nearly killed by members of an American infantry squad who thought he was a Viet Cong.

"Your Papa is very sick, not the same."

There is a detached melancholia to Mama's manner; she's not the passionate and aggressive woman she once was. Le Ly is quietly shocked by her mother's condition.

Le Ly finds Papa sitting inside the house, bruises still apparent, drinking alcohol. Bombs and artillery fire are heard in the distance. She kneels down next to her father.

"Papa, you're drinking now!"

Papa smiles weakly. "That stupid wizard came by the other day.

He said to me, 'I have nothing to tell you.' Just like that—I have no future."

"That's not what he meant. You're just imagining things," Le Ly comforts him.

"What's wrong with living forever with your ancestors?" Papa replies. "I'm worried about you, Bay Ly. The land's going to be yours now—but your Mama is not the same."

Papa relates another terrible story to Le Ly: about how the Viet Cong came back to Ky La after a night battle with the Americans. The young VC captain of years past—now embittered and horribly scarred—took five women from the village and accused them of collaborating with the enemy. Mama was one of them.

One by one, the VC captain walked down the line and killed each of the women with a pistol shot to the head. Finally, it was Mama's turn. But Le Ly's Uncle Luc protested to the captain that no woman who sent two sons to fight and possibly die for the revolution could even think of betraying her country. And so she was spared at the last moment.

Papa sits with Le Ly in front of the village's Buddhist temple, now in ruins. Shaken by the story of what has befallen her mother, Le Ly declares: "I never should have left Ky La. I should have stayed to fight them all—the Viet Cong, the government—what am I now Papa? Not warrior woman, not a Phung. Just a tramp, begging in the streets of the city. I am so ashamed, Papa."

Papa looks into the eyes of his beloved daughter. "Don't be ashamed," he tells her intently. "You did the best you could. You were born to be a wife and a mother, not a killer."

Papa takes Le Ly into his arms.

"No, my little Bay Ly, don't ask what is right or wrong. These questions are very dangerous. Right is only the goodness you carry in your heart—love for your ancestors and your family. Wrong is all that comes between you and that love. Go back to your son. Make him the best son you can! That is the war you must fight! That is the victory you must win."

Papa senses a neighbor coming. "Now go, quick, before they see you and talk," he tells Le Ly.

She knows that this is the last time she will ever see her Papa. Tears flood her eyes. How can she leave him?

Watching Le Ly walk away, Papa finally breaks. She runs back into his arms one last time. "My little peach blossom," he whispers, "what will you do without me?"

Le Ly's father dies soon thereafter. "My father taught me to live and not to die," she says. "He taught me by doing—by forgiving me for being unwed and taking to his heart my little child. I bought my father the best funeral he could have and we mourned him for one hundred days. Raising my only son became my purpose in life."

Another year passes. Le Ly is now working for tips at the Korean Commissary in Da Nang. Attractively dressed in a purple *ao dai* and riding her Honda scooter down a crowded street, she's flagged down by a tough bargirl friend, who's accompanied by a tall, rugged-looking, older American Marine dressed in fatigues and aviator glasses.

Le Ly's friend introduces her to the Marine, Sergeant Steve Butler. In Vietnamese, the bargirl tells Le Ly, "Look, he wants to meet a nice Vietnamese girl, yes? I can't take him home. I do not need another man in my life now. You go with him and give him good time."

Le Ly looks into Steve's face. Unlike younger, impatient American men, he simply lights a cigarette, smiles, and waits. His eyes are kind, worldly.

"No. I don't do that. I have bad luck with men, you know that," Le Ly tells her friend.

"Look, Ly—he already gave me the money. I can't give it back. I got five kids. I need the cash!"

"Sorry," Le Ly responds, and begins to rev up her bike. "Wait!" says her friend. "Let me tell him you agreed, okay? He'll give me the rest of the money he promised, then we take off! He's too old to run after both of us. What do you say?"

"Okay," Le Ly agrees. "Get ready to run." And with that, the bargirl says something in Steve's ear, takes another slew of American greenbacks from him, and, snapping her purse shut, darts down the street. Le Ly takes off in the opposite direction on her scooter. Steve hesitates, not knowing which woman to chase. He decides to go after Le Ly.

Le Ly rides quickly through the market with Steve in pursuit, then stops in a small café for a drink, thinking she's lost the Marine. There she spies Steve riding in the front of a siclo cab, combing the neighborhood for her. She heads for a rear exit.

Le Ly slips out of the bar, only to notice Steve calmly waiting for her in front of her apartment building.

"Hi . . . sorry," Le Ly tells him, in English. "My friend not to take no for an answer. You chase her, not me. Not my fault. Sorry."

She takes out her key, but as Le Ly opens the door Steve is still standing there. "Yes? You want something else?" she asks him. "You want girl, go see hooker, don't bother me, okay?"

"I'm a little too old for a hooker," Steve laughs. "I just wanted to meet you. I don't care about the money. Your friend introduced us and that's all I wanted. Now—since I've gone to all this trouble—may I come in and talk to you for a moment?"

Feeling guilty, Le Ly allows him to enter, but with a warning: "One minute, I leave door open. You bad guy, one funny move, I call police. I good girl."

In her apartment, neither Le Ly nor Steve quite know what to say to each other. Then Steve's minute is up. "Okay, thank you for coming," she says abruptly. "I go work now. Good-bye. I hope you happy stay in Da Nang."

"I'll be happy to wait for you till you come back," he says affably.

"No, I go long time. I work Korean casino. Serve booze. Hostess."

"That's perfectly all right. I have no place to go. Besides, I gave all my money to your friend. I can't even pay for a taxi out of here. Tell you the truth, I'm kind of tired from our little race."

Le Ly is feeling guilty again. "Okay," she tells Steve. "You stay—not too long—okay? When you go, lock door please."

"Maybe we can have dinner later?" he asks.

"No. I have dinner. Not possible. I be back long time."

"That's no problem," Steve responds.

"No. Lock door when you go. Nice meeting you. Good-bye." And she's gone.

When Le Ly returns much later that night, she's astonished to discover Steve sitting up in her bed.

"Hi. I hope you don't mind if I stretched out for a minute. That chair got kind of uncomfortable."

"What? You're still here?" she nearly shouts.

"Well, you said I could rest. And I do want to take you to dinner, to thank you for your hospitality."

"You no understand! I no want to go to dinner. Me no want boyfriend!"

"Do you have a boyfriend?" he asks her.

"You *dinky dau*. No—no boyfriend now. Me had boyfriend but me no want new boyfriend."

"I'm sorry. It sounds like he must've hurt you very much." Steve seems genuinely concerned.

"Look, you want me to give you money for taxi?" she finally inquires.

"No," Steve responds. "I'm perfectly happy right here."

"I know you want stay here, but this is my house. You want a woman, I call siclo driver find you girl for tonight."

"I told you I'm not interested in prostitutes," Steve tells Le Ly. "I'm interested in you."

What is Le Ly going to do with this man? What does he want?

Steve picks up a framed photograph of Hung.

"Is this your little brother?"

"My son," she says.

"Oh, of course," Steve smiles. "He looks just like you! Lots of spirit around the eyes!" He puts the picture down carefully, like a treasure. His eyes linger on a stolen photograph of Anh. Le Ly catches his look, sensing something sad and different about Steve.

"I'm sorry," she tells him "Me not very nice to you. You like some tea?"

They talk and talk through a rainy night. Steve shows Le Ly some pictures of his own family. American rock and roll plays in the background on a radio.

When Steve notices that Le Ly has become tired, he stands up and says, "I'll leave you alone now."

"No," she says. "Too much rain. No taxi. You stay till no more rain."

The rain continues outside. Steve, a blanket covering him on the floor, is mumbling to himself in sleep. Le Ly watches him.

Steve kicks his legs, waves his arms, in the grip of a terrible nightmare. She comes to him, his eyes pop open—alert, terrified. His eyes pull her in. He begins kissing her. They make quiet love, two lonely, lost people finding another soul to cling to.

One week later, Steve walks into Le Ly's apartment, loaded down with an armful of bags. "Just a few things for you and your family." He beams. "Come on, we'll have Christmas all over again."

Le Ly protests. "You cannot do this." But Steve is adamant. "Oh, yes I can! Look, Le Ly, I'm not very good with words. Even if I spoke your language, I don't think I could tell you how I feel. I just want a little peace and happiness, okay? I just want to be with you and help you—and your little boy and your mom, too."

"I no want to be your girlfriend, Steve," she answers. "Me have bad luck with men. Me have bad karma, you understand? You find better girl."

Steve holds steady. "Listen, I know all about karma," he says firmly. "Mine has taken me all over the world for most of my life! Living out of a duffel bag. It's time for me to settle down, to quit pretending I'm going to live forever. I'm going home to San Diego. I got a family and a house there.

"I want you, Ly . . . to be there with me. You'll be safe, you'll be free, your boy will have an education. My first wife taught me a real lesson in my life. I need a good Oriental woman like you. If you'll have me, I want you to be my wife."

Her heart melts in the face of Steve's gentle yearning. He is literally offering her and her child the world, *his* world. It will be difficult to say no to his offer.

One year later, it is Christmas 1968 in the beautiful mountain town of An Khe, in Vietnam's Central Highlands. Le Ly is living in a large, spacious, and, by her standards, luxurious house on a military base with Steve, Hung, and their new baby, Tommy. Mama visits her daughter, the somewhat strange American, and the two children. Steve announces to Mama that they're Americanizing Hung's name to Jimmy.

After dinner, Mama and Le Ly sit on a porch overlooking a beautiful valley. The calm and silence are punctuated with occasional weapon fire and the roar of armored vehicles guarding the perimeter of the base.

"Your Papa wanted you to stay on the land," Mama firmly tells her daughter.

"I can't Mama, I can't . . . it's the past . . . "

"Who will take care of the land? I am old."

"Hai . . . and maybe Bon will come back. I know he will," says Le Ly of the brother who left home so many years before.

"Ma . . . In America I can save the children. The South is dying. Steve says it will fall faster than anyone thinks. He has a mother and sister near San Diego, and will leave the army soon to take a good job. He wants me for his wife. He loves me. I love him."

"You love him?" Mama asks piercingly.

Le Ly pauses. "Yes. Steve is good, Mama. He loves the children!"

Mama looks at her daughter intently. "Americans are *thu vo thuy vo chung*—they have no beginning and no end. They do not care about their ancestors, so they think they're free to do any bad thing they want in this life. . . . You will not be happy with this man . . . and your father's spirit will not rest until his most beloved child sleeps in his house."

And without a farewell, Mama rises and goes to bed.

Once more, war intrudes upon Le Ly's life, as An Khe comes under furious attack by North Vietnamese forces. Le Ly, with Tommy and Jimmy in her arms, runs from the house, artillery shells hitting everywhere.

Suddenly a helicopter is right above her, blasting wind. Steve jumps out of the chopper, the blades whipping the wind.

"Come on," he orders Le Ly. "No time." His eyes are red-rimmed, his face grimy and unshaven, his voice hoarse. With him is a Marine buddy, Larry, trying to hurry Steve up.

Steve hoists Le Ly and the two children onto the cordite floor of the helicopter, then jumps up and gives the pilot the signal to lift off—but not before he stuffs a note into Le Ly's purse: "To Whom It May Concern: Help this family get out of Vietnam. Reward. Gunnery Sergeant Steve Butler, U.S.M.C."

Later, the chopper descends near a river and highway at Qui Nhon, a long four-hundred-twenty miles north of Saigon. "Okay, miss," the door gunner tells Le Ly. "End of the line."

"But Saigon? You take us to Saigon?" she yells above the roar of the rotors. The crewman only shakes his head and climbs back in, as Le Ly and the children scurry to get out of the range of the chopper blast.

As the helicopter flies off, Le Ly is astonished by the sight of thousands of refugees, vehicles, animals, all streaming south toward Saigon in an effort to escape the increasingly victorious North Vietnamese Army and Viet Cong forces.

Le Ly, Jimmy, and Tommy merge into this anonymous tide of humanity surging toward what they hope will be the last bastion of safety in Vietnam.

Le Ly finally makes it to Saigon on an old creaking bus. Fighting a hysterical mob at an American military office, she shows Steve's note to a harried staff sergeant. "He's listed as missing in action, ma'am," he informs Le Ly. "I'm sorry. Check back tomorrow."

Le Ly is staggered by this news. Blankly, she walks onto a crowded street with Jimmy and Tommy. The city has gone mad. Profiteers, soldiers everywhere, a frenzied wheeze of corruption before the storm.

She walks on, lost, holding one child, trailing the other.

Suddenly, as if in dream, he's there, across the street, coming towards her—Steve, her savior, maybe the love of her life. She can't believe it.

That jaunty smile, the cocksure walk, the grimy jungle fatigues and boots—he's obviously just made it back from somewhere missing in action as he gives her a cock of the hand . . . it's you, babe.

Tommy and Jimmy run over and grab Steve's legs. "Sergeant Daddy," Tommy cries. In moments, Le Ly is in Steve's arms. They crush each other with kisses, and the two boys cling to their embrace.

The city swirls around this little circle, a city heading toward the abyss, wending its way toward the inevitable conclusion of a confused, chaotic war.

But Steve and Le Ly are already somewhere else.

AMERICA

The suburbs of San Diego, California. It is 1972. Le Ly, wearing a beautiful *ao dai,* drives up with her handsome Marine husband in full uniform and two kids in the rear.

"Well, here it is, babe," Steve grins. "The dream begins."

Standing in front of their ranch-style house are Eugenia and Bernice, Steve's mother and sister, and a gaggle of little dogs yapping at their feet.

"Mom, she's here!" Bernice shrieks. "Ohhh! She's so cute—like a little China doll! I want to hug her to pieces!"

Le Ly bows low in the traditional Vietnamese greeting when Bernice, fulfilling her promise, pulls the smaller woman into her beefy arms.

"And the children!" shouts Bernice upon spying Tommy and Jimmy in the car. "Ooooo—I can't wait. I just want to eat them up!"

The family walks into their new house. And what a home—such a contrast to Le Ly's austere, hand-built Ky La residence. The furniture is for the most part sealed with plastic. Floral patterns dominate a mixture of antique and tacky mod-erama.

"Not bad, huh?" says Steve proudly. "We'll be here just a while, honey. But soon we'll get a place of our own, I promise."

Le Ly, thinking they *did* have a place of their own, is surprised, but she doesn't say anything while Steve banters with Bernice and Eugenia.

That night, Le Ly is introduced to one of America's wonders: the inside of a typical refrigerator. She gets the guided tour from Bernice: "Steak, peas, potatoes, and for dessert—strawberries! We'll have you and the kids back to normal in no time."

Le Ly is puzzled by the notion of food that's frozen rather than bought in the market on a daily basis.

Later at dinner, Le Ly tries to navigate her way through the usage of a knife and fork, held like pencils, then jiggled like acrobats between hands when it's time to cut. Eugenia tells Steve that his ex-wife, Beverly, has been calling. Steve drinks so much during dinner that he actually mispronounces Le Ly's name.

A few days later, Steve and Le Ly drive into a supermarket parking lot in a beat-up automobile. "Think of it as a Saigon taxi," he tells her. "Just a rental—my personal vehicle's in the shop."

"Steve, you know I understand about money—you in the Marines long time and you still live with your mother?"

"The problem's Beverly," Steve defends himself. "Got half my paycheck plus support for the two kids and she's still pissed. I'm just about bankrupt, Ly."

He parks. A feeling of dread comes over Le Ly.

"I just got three more years; I'll get out with a good pension," Steve reassures her. After that I got a civilian job waiting—the big bucks—the two of us. We'll be back in the Far East—Indonesia, Singapore. I'll be making seventy-five thousand a year. Guaranteed, promised to me."

"What is this job, Steve?"

"Well, I can't tell you, Ly. Not just yet. It's confidential, but it's gonna work out."

Inside the supermarket, Le Ly is introduced to yet another magic kingdom. She's never seen anything like this. A warehouse of food, in all shapes and packages.

They stop near the rice shelves, filled with different labels and pictures of instant rice.

"Pick one!" Steve invites her.

Overwhelmed by the choices of instant rice—the grain that used to take months to plant and harvest in Ky La—Le Ly opts for Uncle Ben's. "Uncle is trusted man," she reasons.

At the checkout counter, Steve teaches Le Ly how to pay by check. She notices the hateful stare of a young woman clerk. "They don't get it, Ly," he comforts his wife. "I do. We'll lick 'em together."

Le Ly spends her first Thanksgiving at Eugenia's house with extended members of the Butler family and Steve's old war buddy, Larry. Le Ly's welcome into the family has already become somewhat worn out. Bernice thinks Le Ly lives in her own dreamworld, and is taking Steve for a ride.

During the meal, everyone eats voraciously except for Le Ly, who finds the turkey tough and dry. "Come on, Le Ly, it's Thanksgiving," Bernice admonishes her. "Think of all those starving children in Vietnam."

"Oh, Bernice, leave the poor girl alone," says Eugenia. "She always eats like a sparrow."

"Yeah, rice and fish, fish and rice," complains Bernice. "That's all the kids get. They're starving for some good old-fashioned meat and potatoes!"

"They more loving when they stay with parents," she explains. "Who else protects them from evil spirits that—"

"Ly, it ain't Vietnam in this bedroom. It's California. Kids sleep by themselves. It makes them independent."

Le Ly moves closer to Steve, says to him, "You Le Ly hero, tonight you protect Le Ly. You good man."

"Ah, just too much whiskey," he says, and begins making love to her. She stops him tenderly.

"Steve, I go work. I want make money. I want get out here, out house. I think your family like their dogs better than our boys."

"What would you do, anyway?" Steve asks her quizzically.

"Work factory. Restaurant. They plenty of Oriental restaurants growing around here."

"I wish I could go back to 'Nam," Steve replies, not liking her idea. "Make a bundle. Tell you the truth, I kind of miss it in a way."

"Steve, what they want you do for so much money make you wait so much time now?"

Steve pauses. "Well, this is just between you and me, okay? The government's got rules about the kinds of jobs you can take after what I done and this one's . . . sensitive."

"What is this job?" Le Ly presses Steve. "You trust me? Yes?"

"Arms . . . selling arms."

Le Ly stops moving.

"I don't understand. You joking."

"What do you think I been doing for the last seventeen years? What do you think a military adviser does? I go into countries the US is helping and teach 'em to use the weapons our corporations sell."

Le Ly is stunned, uncomprehending. "You been doing that for seventeen years?"

"Yeah. But as a civilian, I'll make money on the weapons themselves instead of just a crummy Marine paycheck. That's why this is sensitive—'cause the government doesn't want 'tops' taking jobs with major contractors right after they retire."

Le Ly bolts upright in bed. "You sell guns to governments so that they can go blow up women and children!"

"Don't get on your high horse," Steve cautions her. "I knew you wouldn't understand."

"I understand as well as anybody," she insists. "Remember who you talking to?"

Now Steve is angry. "Then you goddamn well know that if we

76

didn't sell arms to these people the fuckin' communists would! Then how would they be any better off?"

"Guns, communists!" Le Ly shouts. "Is that all anybody in America ever thinks about?"

"It's my life, Ly, it's all I know how to do. At least I'll get paid more for doing it."

Le Ly looks at her husband, not quite knowing him anymore. "Don't you ever hear anything Le Ly ever tell you?"

"You mean the Buddha stuff," he says with some exasperation.

"Not just that . . . but about my family, my life! We don't know anything about each other! You lie to me in Vietnam."

Le Ly, caught between rage and sorrow, turns away from her husband.

"Well, it wasn't a lie, exactly," he says weakly. "It was a white lie—a good lie. C'mon, baby . . . don't do this . . . I love you, honey, I love you."

Time passes, and Le Ly becomes more determined to make it in America her way. She works first on the assembly line in a San Diego factory, making circuit boards with other Vietnamese women. She then segues to a position as the hostess at a Chinese restaurant, negotiating with the owner for a loan. She wants to lease a Vietnamese delicatessen and start her own business. Le Ly, with increased business acumen, argues with its landlord over the rent.

Steve, drinking more than ever and unhappy with his job at the Marine base, is slowly unraveling. He and Le Ly fight incessantly. They now live in a small house of their own in El Cajon, and have a new son, two-year-old Alan. Jimmy is now eight, and Tommy is six. They play with toy guns as an episode of "I Love Lucy" plays on the TV.

Steve refuses to sign the lease for Le Ly's delicatessen. "Fine, Steve. No sign," she snaps, irritated. "I continue without your signature. I put up more money for the insurance, okay?"

"You don't know what you're getting into, Ly! I don't want you doing this."

"Why not?" she asks. "What can I lose?"

"What can we lose? I'll tell you: our house, our cars, the school money—everything! What if the potato salad goes bad and everyone gets sick! You don't know Americans like I do. They sue at the drop of a hat. Besides, you're just a dumb immigrant. Lawyers'll skin you alive."

Le Ly argues that other Vietnamese own stores.

"Yeah, because they're refugees and the government backs their loans. You're not a refugee, you got a white man behind you and there's nobody to protect me if you get into trouble. Goddamn expenses are killing us, honey. Just laid out a hundred and seventy-five dollars for a new paint job, new clothes for the baby—"

"—and the guns," she puts in quickly, referring to his ever-increasing collection of weaponry.

"Rent, food for five, and Buddha here—" Steve points to the Vietnamese household shrine she carefully maintains in the spirit of her traditions—"sucks up more candles than a five-alarm fire. Got the whole damned family staring at me all the time," he complains, referring to the photographs of Le Ly's father, brother, and other family members that adorn the shrine.

Le Ly is stung by Steve's insult to her ways. "Steve, you agree it's important for the children to know their family, respect their ancestors."

"Yeah, well, Alan and Tommy are going to catechism starting next week," announces Steve triumphantly. "And what the hell you do with Jimmy, that's your business."

Their argument escalates. Steve complains about Le Ly's cooking. She complains about his drinking and gun collection. Steve, in a theological snit, refers to Le Ly's Buddha as a "goddamn devil."

"Buddha no devil," she says, standing her ground.

"Well, he's a graven image—a golden calf—read the Bible and you'll see. He was just a man. You can't worship just a man!"

"I don't worship him," says Le Ly, fighting Steve off. "I only offer prayers and respect."

"You really need to read your Bible," he tells her. "'Cause your Buddha don't know shit! Heathens! In my fucking house! Have I gone nuts or what!"

Bernice and Eugenia, who happen to be visiting, both witness the argument. Eugenia takes Le Ly aside, and tells her gently but firmly, "Don't ever shout at my son like that again. He's going through a bad time is all, and he needs your support, not your anger, girl."

The next morning, Le Ly awakens to find that Steve has taken her car keys and credit cards. Later, he takes her car as well, in an attempt to gain complete control over his wife. Le Ly gives up the deli and loses ten thousand dollars to the landlord in the process.

Conditions worsen between Le Ly and Steve. They argue about money, but he still spends more of it on weapons.

"Why spend four hundred dollars on two more guns, Steve? Why?" she asks her husband on a rainy night

"Don't you get it? Are you still bitching about money! That's the little gook in you!" he spits out, insulting Le Ly as he handles his extensive gun collection. "These goddamn guns are worth something. I can sell them right now and make twice what I got in 'em! One day they might be the only thing that stands between you and death!"

"Death from who?" she asks. "You the only person who waves a gun around here! You the only person who drinks and shoots!"

"Not from me, baby. From dinks! Sappers! After you've wined and dined 'em to take what they've seen."

"What you talking about, dinks?" Le Ly is frightened at Steve's illogical behavior. "You not in Vietnam anymore!"

"Oh yeah?" he responds, emotions escalating. "I don't need you telling me what I should have and shouldn't have. They're my sons too. I'm going to take 'em into the mountains and teach 'em how to hunt and shoot. They gonna learn what it takes to survive in this world."

Le Ly blows up. "No way! You will not teach my children to use guns! I see too many guns in my life! Killing no way to protect anything! I don't want them in my house! If you want them, you get out!"

Now husband and wife face off, not like a couple but like enemies from opposite sides of the world.

"Don't you ever tell me to get outta my own goddamn house! I read your goddamn letter, ya lying little gook!"

"What letter?" she asks, stunned.

"The one written by your dink lover. I saw it—stashed in your purse. What the fuck's he writing you in Vietnamese about. He wants you back?"

"No! Anh just ask about Jimmy. I send picture—"

"Bullshit! You lying little bitch!" he brutally cuts her off.

Calming, Le Ly says, "Steve—I think one time I love you. But I see now we are too different inside to be soulmate. No more mistakes now—not with children so young."

Steve is flabbergasted. "Are you saying—you want to divorce me? Is that what you're saying, Ly?"

She pauses. "If I learn one thing, Steve, in a marriage, no such thing as one happy person. If one miserable, both miserable. That the way life work."

82

"No, baby . . . *this* is the way life works!" Steve suddenly jack-hammers his shotgun up to her face, chambering the round, and pointing the barrel directly at Le Ly. Suddenly time stands still. Le Ly sees herself, back at Ky La, a Viet Cong rifle to her head.

But her time has not come yet. Steve suddenly breaks out in great, racking sobs.

"Oh, God, Ly! I can't . . . I can't live without you! They got me so tied up, baby . . . "

"Steve, who is doing this to you?"

"The Marines," he answers bitterly. "I'm not getting the job I promised you. I'm up for an Admin Board. They're going to kick me out. You don't know the half of it, baby."

"Tell me, Steve," she implores him. "You must tell me."

Steve dissolves in front of her eyes, this strong, handsome man losing himself in memory.

"I'm a killer, baby. I killed so many over there . . . I got so good at it, they reassigned me to the projects . . . black ops . . . and we

killed . . . sometimes three, four a night—all kinds, rice farmers, rich fat cats bankrolling VC units. It was a mind fuck, psyops, knives—rip a man's guts out . . . take a bite out of his liver and then drop it on his chest so he can't get into Buddha heaven and leave 'em in the road . . . or cut his nuts off, stuff 'em in his mouth and sew up his lips like Frankenstein and leave him in his bed in his house."

Le Ly is horrified, hypnotized by her husband's confession.

"I didn't care," he continues, unable to stop himself. "Drugs, running guns, slavery, you name it. One time this guy killed a gook girl I was shacking with because we weren't supposed to fraternize with any Viet nationals outside channels. So they killed her—slashed her throat from ear to ear. I was in hell, baby, our hell. Maybe I went *dinky dau,* maybe I am nuts—who the fuck knows!

"The more I killed, the more they gave me to kill. Do you know what it's like doing that? It's like being eaten inside out by a bellyful of sharks. You gotta keep moving, you gotta keep hitting, 'cause if you stop, the fuckin' sharks'll eat you alive."

He pauses.

"One day they cut me off. Then I met you. It all changed. Or so I thought—but, baby, nothing ever changes, so fuck *me*!"

Impulsively, Steve brings the gun to his mouth . . .

. . . And Le Ly grabs hold of the rifle, not knowing what to do, what to say.

"I'm sorry, I'm sorry," Steve cries. "I could never tell you. I'm scared to death."

"I don't know, Steve," she says. "I too was a soldier in past lives. I hurt many people. I lie, I steal, I hate. Now I pay. We are the same, Steve, we have made very bad karma . . . one day our soul debt will come due, if not in this life then another. But we can't give up."

Steve, pathetic, asks imploringly, "Ly . . . can you love me? Can you really love me?" He buries his head in her breast, crying like a baby. She takes the gun from his hand and puts it down. In her way, she forgives him. But it is not for her to forgive everything.

As time passes, Steve's situation worsens. He becomes more erratic, sinks more deeply into the morass of his past, unable to make peace with the present. It is time for Le Ly to take action.

On a gray California day, Steve loads his things into a van with Larry's help. The marriage is over . . . but the war is just beginning.

Although legally he's supposed to stay away from the house, Steve shows up one Sunday—unshaven, alcoholic signs around his eyes—and announces that he's taking Alan and Tommy to Mass. Le Ly tries to stop him, then follows with Jimmy.

"What are you doing?" demands Steve.

"We're going with you," says Le Ly, frightened for the welfare of her other two boys.

"No, you're not! You stay right goddamn here and fix lunch."

Le Ly forces herself into Steve's van. He stands on the curb, glaring at her through the windshield.

"Bitch!" he hisses.

Slamming his fist on the hood, Steve comes around to get into the driver's seat, though neither he nor Le Ly are dressed for services.

After Mass, Steve sweeps out the church door with the children in tow, on his way to the playground next door. Le Ly runs toward them, her vision blocked by the milling parishioners. When she gets to the playground, only Jimmy is visible. Steve, Tommy, and Alan are nowhere in sight.

Le Ly's phone rings. It's Steve. Her breath catches in her throat.

"Steve? How is Alan? Tommy?"

"They're fine, " he says from a pay phone. "Do you want to see them again?"

"Of course! I'm worried sick. The police are looking every-where for you."

"Fuck the police," he retaliates. "If you want to see them again, do exactly what I tell you."

Le Ly is terrified of Steve's calmness. "What do you want?"

"Write a letter to that bitch lawyer of yours. Tell her you're dropping all charges against me. Tell her you want the house and all our stuff put into my name. Tell her you're dropping the divorce. Do you hear me?"

Le Ly is breaking. "Don't hurt the children," she begs him. "Don't . . . "

Beside herself, Le Ly seeks comfort from her monk in a small Buddhist temple. The converted house is filled with statues of the

Buddha, the main altar radiating electric pulses of light like a spiritual amusement park.

Le Ly is filled with rage. "My boys! I had them heavy in my belly. I birthed them with pain. I am shocked, I am insulted at the insolence of men. All American men I have known become narrow, angry, full of vengeance. I cannot believe such men have known a mother's love! They have no awareness of the sacred origins of life. They have no idea where they come from or where they are going, they love their guns more than their ancestors—and why not! They're nothing but dogs themselves!

But the monk's response is more gentle and compassionate.

"In the war you saw many people killed—old women, babies. Were these people blameless?"

"I don't know master," Le Ly answers.

"So when I show you a little baby run through on a bayonet and say it is his karma, we may cry for the baby—for the baby's karma and the bad karma made by the soldier who killed it—but we must never use our grief to deny the wheel of incarnation that caused the act. It is as natural as the movements of the sun and moon."

Le Ly is resolute. "Master, I want to break this bond of debt with Steve as soon and as cleanly as possible. I don't want to have to repeat this lesson in my next life. How can I explain to him we must be friends and soulmates without being husband and wife?"

"He has created much soul debt for himself," the monk says. "But if you fail to give him the opportunity to redeem himself, you will only increase your own soul debt. The man-hate that blinds you will blind any mate you find in a future life. If you turn Steve away, you will be rejecting your own redemption.

"Child," continues the monk, "you have forgiven the men who raped you, destroyed your country, harmed your family—and this is how it should be. Do not add more man-hate on your shoulders. Your karma is mixed with Steve's to Tommy and Alan. The future, the past are all the same. You divorce, you will only have to come back again and work it out. What you do now affects them both. The path to nirvana is steep and narrow. Choose well, peach blossom . . ."

Le Ly looks up, as if her father is talking to her. How does this monk know her father's most intimate name for her?

The monk smiles. "A child without a father is like a house without a roof."

That night, Le Ly's phone rings again. It's her sister Kim, who is also living in the United States with her GI husband, Bert. "Ly—listen carefully! Steve and the two boys are here now—yes, with Bert. They're drinking . . . they're so drunk! He's getting ready to take them to Canada. The boys are very upset and don't want to stay with Steve anymore—"

"Please! Kim, put Steve on. I must speak to him!" pleads Le Ly.

There is a listening silence on the other end. Le Ly realizes Steve is there.

"Steve . . . Please! I know you hate me, but . . . I don't hate you. Let me help you. Let me try . . . I feel your pain. Forgive me, Steve, for my cruelty.

"You come back home. No police. Just you, me, the children. We make this right. We try. I will go to your church. I will try harder.

I put the shrine away. I work harder to understand you. I love you, Steve. I love the man I saw in Vietnam. I find you again . . . He still there, Steve. I still love you."

Steve clumsily puts the phone down, an ineffable sadness in his face. Le Ly's redemptive feelings shame him.

Le Ly, hearing the dial tone after Steve has hung up, tears out of the house toward her sister's apartment.

Night rain. Le Ly pulls up, sees the police cars with their whirling lights. Then Kim, running to embrace her. "What! Tell me!" Le Ly demands.

"They're all right. Steve—Steve . . . "

"What? What?"

"He kill himself . . . "

Le Ly, beyond horror, walks to Steve's van. Inside, Steve is sprawled across the steering wheel, naked, shards of the shattered window and his own blood everywhere.

Le Ly intercepts her children before they can see their father and furiously hugs them, sharing what's left of her reedy strength.

In Le Ly's house, incense and candles burn on the shrine, with offerings to pictures of Steve. The drapes are drawn, the room plunged in dark candlelight.

A local wizard, a wispy little old Vietnamese man with a gray beard, giggles. "The spirits are here," he announces to Le Ly. "Oh, there are so many of them I can't believe it. Oh, this is marvelous!"

He pauses.

"Ly, Steve is here. He's a little shy. He doesn't want to come into the house. He's not used to this new world. He's bitter—yes, but he forgives you. He's in much pain—so much untold when he died—a soul must leave this earth as naked as it came. He wants—he asks—for you to take his soul to the Buddhist temple. He wants to be close to your love. As he finds peace, so will your family—his descendants—find peace."

"Are you sure that was Steve?" Le Ly asks incredulously. "He was such a strong Christian."

"Steve is surprised now about a lot of things," the monk says

cheerily. "Trust me . . . he's changed a lot. And by the way, this house . . ."

"What?" asks Le Ly anxiously.

"Have to leave. No good. Your front door lines up with your back door. Everything that comes into your life the front way will go out the back: men, money, happiness, everything."

Le Ly knows that this strange, wizened man speaks the truth.

VIETNAM

The jetliner moves high over the Vietnamese earth, high over the verdant rice fields, craggy peaks, winding rivers. Sitting at a window in the Vietnam Airlines plane is Le Ly, now nearing forty years of age. It is 1986. And she is returning home with her three children. But home to what? It has been such a long time.

Le Ly, through faith, tenacity, and indomitable spirit, has transcended all of the incredible trials of her life to become a successful American businesswoman. Now, she is returning to Vietnam, searching for reconciliation with her past and her family.

Her journey of rediscovery begins with a stop in Saigon, now renamed Ho Chi Minh City by the new order that rules from the North, and a visit to Anh— her aristocratic lover, and the father of Jimmy.

Anh's handsome face has aged with time. There are now bags below his eyes and sagging skin beneath the once sharp line of his jaw. Toothpick legs and rubber sandals speak of a man reduced from power and wealth to poverty.

He stands in front of a small cotton-weaving factory, where he now works. Anh and Le Ly embrace with the memory of love, and the friendship of time. Anh breaks from the lingering embrace to see his son Hung—now the teenaged

American boy, Jimmy. Tommy and Alan stand nearby. Anh and Jimmy recognize each other without introduction. The young man smiles at Anh and says "*Chao ba*" the traditional Vietnamese greeting to a respected elder.

Anh chokes back his tears, then reaches out and hugs his son to his chest. Le Ly is moved beyond her wildest hopes.

Now it is time for another, even more important reunion. It has been so many long, eventful years since Le Ly last saw her mother. Now she and her three sons walk through Ky La, so different, so unchanged since she left. Groups of village children follow this elegantly dressed woman, yelling excitedly. Dogs bark. Little girls tend ducks, just as Le Ly did when she was their age. The village has been rebuilt, much of the old gray and brown stone replaced with more colorful concrete façades.

But Le Ly's house is there, finally at peace. Relatives and family yell out, greeting her and the boys.

And then Mama, old and gnarled, is standing by the well, straining through her failing eyesight to recognize her daughter.

"Mama . . . Mama," whispers Le Ly, standing at a little distance.

Mama's bony hands pull the kerchief from her brittle gray hair, her dark eyes now transfixing her daughter with a look of surprise. Her betel-black lips stay sealed as if not really recognizing her daughter.

"Mama," Le Ly repeats, and freezes, so as not to frighten this old woman, whose eyes are scanning Le Ly from top to bottom.

"Bay Ly?" Mama finally says hoarsely.

Le Ly inches closer toward embrace.

"You look healthy," says Mama. "How is your sister Kim?"

"Fine . . . fine . . . These are your grandsons, Mama—my boys. Hung is now called Jimmy. This is Tommy . . . and this is Alan, who was born in America."

Mama looks proudly at her three grandsons and hugs them all—but there's no embrace for Le Ly.

Mama speaks a few words of Vietnamese with her grandchildren, difficult for them to understand. Older sister Hai, looking gnarled as a mangrove root, approaches skeptically. She's accompanied by a man in his forties; this is brother Bon, unseen by Le Ly since he and Sau were taken away to fight for the North in the mists of time.

Bon walks up to Le Ly. She knows who it is now, by instinct. He has the authoritative look of a bureaucrat. He shakes hands cordially with Le Ly, bowing in the manner of a relative.

A duck and pig have been slaughtered and cooked for the welcoming feast. Incense drifts from shrines displaying pictures of Papa and brother Sau, as well as various other kin. Mama rattles on, asking the boys questions in translated Vietnamese, broken English, and sign language.

Mama, chewing one of Le Ly's chocolate gifts, offers one to Bon.

"I'm sorry, Mother. I can't."

"Don't spoil the party," Mama chides her son. "I have my oldest son and youngest daughter back with me. My two halves on either side."

"Two halves, maybe," responds Bon, "but from two different worlds. Bay Ly's a capitalist, I'm a communist."

"But you've found common ground at this table," Mama stresses.

"We share the same mother, I agree," says Bon, "and I love her as a sister. But I cannot accept her gifts."

Le Ly, conciliatory, says, "You know, Bon, I had this terrible fear you would despise me because I married your enemy and left the country while you were still fighting."

Bon is touched. "It's been so many years, Bay Ly, much is forgiven, but you have no idea of the suffering the Americans have caused here. Things were very hard. All we had to hold on to was the future, and because we knew that future wouldn't arrive unless we won, we kept dying no matter what, like ants beneath the elephant's feet."

Bon's emotions rise. "It wasn't because we were brave but because we had no choice. Our freedom was all—all that mattered! And when the future finally came, it was more war—the Cambodians, the Chinese. When I came to look for Mama in 1980 you have no idea how much she suffered. She was too old to work the paddies and she had to give the land—our land—to the state after the liberation. When I found Mama and Hai, they were starving. Packs of wild dogs

attacked and bit them. Nobody in the village cared for them. They were just two old ladies scavenging and growing vegetables to stay alive.

"Now, you come here, a rich strange foreigner. You will turn the village once more against them . . . against us, the Phungs, who have suffered so much."

"Things were bad for everyone after liberation," Mama adds. "No one was safe outside their home. '*Troi dat doi thay*'—many times Heaven and Earth changed places."

"If you ask me," chimes in Hai bitterly, "rebuilding a nation after a war is like trying to start a family by getting raped."

"If war produces one thing," says Mama with finality, "it's many cemeteries . . . and in cemeteries, there are no enemies."

It is later in the hot, humid Central Vietnamese afternoon. The men nap. Women clean up. Children play in the yard.

Mama shuffles over to Le Ly, who meditates at the shrine of her father and dead brother. The portrait of Papa gazes down impassively, immortal.

Looking at Sau's picture, Mama's eyes moisten.

"All I could think of for so long was how I made your brother Sau go to war. Your father wanted your poor brother to know some of the joys of married life, but I said no—so sure I was doing the right thing. I gave up a grandson to gain a soldier—and I lost both. How wrong I was."

"It was also Sau's choice," Le Ly reminds her.

"No. He was just being a good son when he obeyed me. If I could, I would've stopped you from going to America. And what would've happened to your sons here?"

Le Ly is touched by her mother's words.

"I'm so proud of you, Bay Ly," says Mama to her daughter. "You've seen the side of things that's hidden from most people."

Le Ly throws her arms around her frail but still radiant mother,

and for the first time since her return, the two women embrace fully, the barriers between them melting away.

"Tears are God's way of paying you back for what he's taken," Mama says. "I have no more tears, I've cried them out to all the directions of the wind. Everything is useless next to just being alive . . . "

Le Ly kisses her mother's face, caresses Mama's hands.

"But you have come back, Bay Ly," Mama continues, "and that's what matters. You have completed your circle of growth. Low tide to high tide, poor to rich, sad to happy, beggar to a fine lady, your past is now complete, and my destiny as your mother is now over. I am looking forward to joining your Papa . . . "

Mama smiles wistfully.

That night Le Ly sleeps in the house her father built with his own hands, in the village that gave her life, and has now infused her with a new path, a new destiny. And her Papa's spirit visits her one final time. There is no need for him to visit her again.

It is day once again in Ky La; Le Ly prays to the Buddha in the little temple. Moving through the graveyard outside, she looks east, she looks west—torn like us all, confused, a product of war and wisdom, peace and love . . . and understanding.

"I have come home, yes, but home has changed and I will always be in-between . . . South-North, East-West, peace-war, Vietnam-America . . . it is my fate to be in-between Heaven and Earth. When we resist our fate, we suffer. When we accept it, we are happy. We have time in abundance—an eternity—to repeat our mistakes, but we need only once correct our mistake—and at last hear the song of enlightenment with which we can break the chain of vengeance forever. In your heart you can hear it now. It's the song your spirit has been singing since the moment of your birth.

"If the monks were right and nothing happens without cause, then the gift of suffering is to bring us closer to God, to teach us to be strong when we are weak, to be brave when we are afraid, to be wise in the midst of confusion, and to let go of that which we can no longer hold.

"Lasting victories are won in the heart . . . not on this land or that."

PART TWO

THE SPIRIT OF HEAVEN AND EARTH

by Le Ly Hayslip with Jay Wurts

Don't let anyone tell you that movies are make believe. Movies possess a spirit, just like the actors in them and the people they portray. These actors walk and talk and have adventures and relive old lives, and, although on screen they are thin as air, the beams of light they ride can penetrate to our hearts. They allow us to see what before we could only imagine. They make the unreal, real. So don't let anyone tell you that Hollywood movies are make believe.

For six months, from August 1992 through January 1993, I helped Oliver Stone and his talented crew bring the ghosts from my past back to life. From as early as 1991, when I first began talking to Oliver about his screenplay, he showed a father's concern not just for the health and appearance of his new off-spring, but for its spirit, too. He knew no story about the Vietnamese could be complete if he showed only our beautiful land and handsome people and all the suffering we'd been through. To tell the whole story, he must also explore the world inside.

When shooting began in Phuket, Thailand, on October 19, 1992, Oliver took me aside and, like my father had done so many years ago, gave me my new mission.

"Ly," he said, "your job as technical advisor will seem very familiar." He jabbed a finger toward my face, "It will be just like going to war! Before we shoot a scene, you tell me if things look okay—the way you remember them or the way they ought to be. After I say *cut,* you tell me how things turned out."

This assignment seemed simple enough. But I soon learned that if I said, "Oh, my father would have looked out the window before he said that—to see if anyone was listening," or "The MPs wouldn't have let those black-market girls so close to the compound," he would call everyone back and re-shoot the scene. After a few of these episodes (and some irritated looks from the hard-working crew), I discovered the difference between comments that truly helped our "off-spring" to grow and those that merely stopped the show. A mother may see many things, but she doesn't necessarily have to tell "papa" everything she saw.

More typically, after an intense scene was over, Oliver would look, at me and if I had tears in my eyes, he would say, "Okay, we got it. Next setup!" I had become the production's official "tear meter." People would simply consult my face the way they looked at light gauges and electrical dials to see if more work was needed. After a while, the spirit of my story had spread to everyone—crew, actors, and extras alike. Even my tears were no longer necessary. The Americans became in their hearts Vietnamese. The Vietnamese became in their hearts American—found themselves viewing their own life stories with new eyes. Physically, everyone gave 200 percent, and our "spiritual gauges" went off the scale. When a scene was good, we would all cry together and everyone knew that the ghost-child to whom we were all godparents was assuming a life of its own.

To prepare for the film, I had taken Oliver, Joan Chen, and young Hiep Thi Le—whom I quickly came to look upon as a daughter—and several members of the crew to my village, Ky La, in Vietnam. Like a thirsty man, Oliver soaked up every detail of village life and asked for more. He met my mother, and in their halting conversation, closely monitored by escorting officials, I saw pass over his face the shadows of ten-thousand mothers and ten-thousand sons who had given themselves to the war. I watched little Hiep become a Ky La farmgirl as she toiled beside her Hollywood Mama Du in the leech-filled paddies behind my old house. When we left the village, we were a family ready to start a great adventure.

This spiritual energy gradually affected everyone on the set in Thailand, where my village and Da Nang of the 1960s had been painstakingly reconstructed. He even asked me and some of the extras to sleep a few nights in the eerily accurate reproduction of my old home so that it would "feel" more lived-in by me and my family's guardian spirits. In fact, we camped on the set for a week.

Since the local Buddhist monks were not empowered to bless the set, Oliver had me say a prayer for luck each morning before we started work. Once, on a very cloudy day, he asked, "Ly, do you think it's going to rain?" He was concerned about finishing an outdoor scene and apparently thought I had some special phone line to Mother Nature.

I replied, grinning, "Give me twenty minutes, okay? I'll go consult my Father!" I said this the way many Vietnamese refer to Mr. Sky, the father of us all. I took a short walk—just to take a break from all the bustle—and saw that the heavy Southeast Asia clouds were a bit too silvery to make us wet—at least very early in the day.

I went back to the set and told Oliver in a joking voice, "The heavens say the rice needs water, but they appreciate your work and will wait until sunset to begin the rain."

Oliver listened to this intently, then turned and shouted orders like a general in battle. After several hours of great activity, the day's shooting was completed just as the first raindrops began to fall.

To this day, I don't know if Oliver took my little joke seriously or if he had simply gotten good at indulging me with a straight face. Of course, I did "consult the heavens" as I said I would, and an old Ky La farmgirl is seldom wrong about the weather. Still, who really knows why Mother Nature does the things she does?

As part of his strict insistence on accuracy and getting at the truth inside the story, Oliver used many non-actor Vietnamese for both featured parts and extras. Most of these people were refugees from what used to be South Vietnam who were driven out by the war and who are now living in Thailand. They all carried with them the spiritual baggage of every refugee: grief for lost loved ones, terrible memories of sights no eyes should see, unutterable longing for their homeland. Their tears spontaneously joined our own, as did their laughter when the script spoke of happier times.

One old man, who was raised in Central Vietnam and had fought on the side of the French in the early 1950s, told me (after performing in the scene where legionnaires burned my father's house) that he now finally realized, near the end of his life, what the war was really like for us peasants.

I think *Heaven and Earth* will have a similar impact on the Americans who see it, especially women. They will be surprised at how much of themselves they see in the young girls and old ladies who used to seem so strange, alien, and exotic. Today, most young women in Vietnam, like most women in America, know about each other only what survivors of the war care to tell them. We are separated not so much by an ocean, but by time and wounded souls.

Of course, as I have learned from my life in the U.S., American women have many advantages over their Vietnamese sisters. They can learn from books, magazines, TV, and movies—and just by looking around!—what women can accomplish: things that most Vietnamese girls cannot, through ignorance, even dream about. As peacetime contact between Vietnam and the United States increases in coming years, both village girls and American women will have a chance to learn other ways of looking at the world. From this new shared perspective, perhaps, we will learn to judge one another not by the standards of our own lives, but by those things shared by women at all times and in all places.

Through this film, too, Americans will learn that the Vietnamese, like themselves, became the way they are because of how they were raised—how they think about themselves, what they believe about others, how they deal with growing up and growing old. They will also see how those views can change. They will learn that introducing two cultures through the matchmaker of war was not the best path to compassion and understanding. If they had a husband or son or brother who went to Vietnam, they will learn a little more about the people who helped or opposed them, and what our land was like before the shells began to fall and the gunfire began to rattle.

In short, when you see this film, you will feel a bond with the people who made it, and through the wonder of this connection, feel new compassion for the people whose lives it depicts.

So don't let anyone tell you that movies are not real. How else can mere flickering light reach so far down into the human soul?

And soul, I believe, is what Oliver's movies are all about. He told me he makes his films the way a father raises a child: doing the best he can to nurture it and make it strong—to give it a sense of humanity and its own life force—then letting it go to find its way in the world. Oliver has given us many strong "sons" this way. I am pleased and honored that, with *Heaven and Earth*, he has now also raised a daughter worthy of his warrior's heart.

Finally, I have been asked many times to compare the movie to the books, *When Heaven and Earth Changed Places* and *Child of War, Woman of Peace*, on which it is based. The best judge of this, of course, is one who experiences them both with fresh eyes, but a mother always has her opinions.

For me, books are an umbilical cord to the mind through which nourishment passes to the heart and soul. The film, however, is like a great warm blanket or a splash in the icy sea. In a darkened theater, it surrounds us and dominates our senses. In the space of minutes we laugh and cry and feel pulse-pounding excitement. All emotions come to the surface—breathtaking beauty and absolute horror, all mixed. While a book gives us time to think about our feelings, a movie makes us feel without giving us time to think. Reflection only comes later. People whose souls are changed by books usually know why. People whose lives are affected by a movie only discover it later on. In this way, movies are very much like life. How can people call them make believe?

Because of this, I ask people who see *Heaven and Earth* to take a few minutes afterward, at a quiet time and place, to think about what they saw and felt. We have shared a journey and witnessed many terrible and wondrous things. Looking over our shoulders, then glancing ahead, we can see that the steep path we have ascended is really a road to a better future.

For the people of modern Vietnam, the war has ended but the blessings of peace have yet to appear. Some two million Vietnamese on both sides were killed during the war, leaving over 130,000 amputees, 300,000 orphans, and an equal number of MIAs behind. Ten percent of South Vietnam's surface area was doused with over seventy-one million liters of toxic chemicals, including eighteen million gallons of Agent Orange. Can you imagine what these chemicals would do to prime farm land in Georgia, California, or Ohio? On top of that, the fifteen-and-a-half million tons of munitions dropped on my country have turned almost fifteen-and-a-half million acres of once-lush tropical forest into desert. Approximately half of Vietnam's children are clinically malnourished, and a little more than that number have dropped out of primary school to scavenge a living as farmers, street kids, and beggars.

The Mother's Love Clinic and Peace Village Medical Center (built near Ky La with Oliver's assistance and sustained with the help of thousands of others) treats some forty thousand patients each year, but this is like a grain of sand on China Beach. Some people, including many Vietnamese government officials, see new and expanded contact with America—even returning Vietnamese-American *Viet Kieu*—as another "foreign invasion." These souls neither think nor feel but only suffer and deserve our compassion. If my books and this movie mean nothing else, it is that the world has seen suffering enough. If the circle of vengeance caused by the Vietnam War—and all wars, everywhere—is ever to be broken, it must certainly begin with us.

COMING FROM THE HEART

by Hiep Thi Le

I must say I am one of the luckiest Asian-Americans because I have been accepted by both sides. Being a part of *Heaven and Earth* was like living in a microcosm with both of my families: the Vietnamese villagers and refugees who taught me to farm and who worked with me on the film in Thailand, and the Americans who produced the movie. The movie brought these two sides of my family together and allowed them to interact. Every encounter and moment I experienced on *Heaven and Earth* helped me become who I am by reinforcing my identity and giving me a sense of what is important to me.

I used to want to belong to a particular race, either Vietnamese or American. But I did not feel I belonged anywhere because I had next to no knowledge or comprehension of either world. If I had to belong to any one group, I would probably be a part of the lost generation of the Asian-Americans.

However, this feeling began to change during my trip back to Vietnam in August of 1992—my first trip back since I left in 1979. A peasant family welcomed Le Ly Hayslip, Joan Chen, and me into their home. They did not know we were working on a movie. All they knew was that Joan and I were to be married to farmers; and we must prove ourselves worthy. We must leave the "city life" and become farmers capable of supporting our future families. I thought farming would be all that I would learn from this family. Little did I know they would teach me that family is what makes me happy.

They showed me that one's background and identity are rooted in one's family. With a family, one can feel contentment and completeness. Living with them and seeing their closeness made me remember my own family. We were separated three ways: some ended up in Hong Kong, some in Vietnam, and my younger sister and I were lost at sea during our search for refuge. I remembered how lonely we were without the family. Even as a lost child, I knew if I could have my family with me, I would be satisfied.

We were finally reunited in the United States after four years of separation. The joy and contentment of that moment made me feel like I had it all and nothing else mattered. I cannot disagree with the farmers who told me that, with one's family, one can overcome many obstacles. The contentment of family erases any need to harm or take vengeance against anyone else because there would be no reason to—there would be no need to. Having a family makes one feel whole and safe.

In Vietnam, family get-togethers are an everyday thing. As they share in the work under the hot sun in their fields, inhabited by snakes and leeches, they perceive it as a family activity. As they work, they make it all fun and games. They make it enjoyable by singing and laughing to cheer each other on. They make life easy and simple.

And in the end, they made me remember what it was like being with my family.

My identity was further reinforced by the Vietnamese refugees in Thailand who were cast as extras. They considered the refugee camps in which they live their home, because they either had spent most of their lives there or were born there. The majority of them were separated from the rest of their families during their escape. Some of them were, like myself, separated from their families at such a young age that they had no knowledge of their parents' names and addresses or hometowns. I remember that when I was at the Hong Kong refugee camp, the captain of the boat took care of my sister and me, and helped us to stand on our own feet. But most refugees had to do everything for themselves. Some adopted each other as family for moral support—the way my sister and I clung onto the captain like he was family. On location, these refugees took care of one another as if they had the same last names.

Prior to working on the movie, I could not understand or figure out how the morals I was taught throughout my life could be applied or how they pertained to me because they all seemed too idealistic. But these refugees actually proved that morals are applicable. For example, during the first week of filming, I came across a seventy-year-old woman who was resting her head on a table. I asked her why she was tired and if she wanted to take some time to recuperate. She explained she had been on a bus for two days and nights, from northern Thailand to the location in Phang-Nga. She added, "I will work until my bones give up on me." Here was this woman, so confident that the two nights' pain and sleeplessness would not slow her down. And she was right! It then dawned on me that I was a poor example of my generation and my family upbringing. I was not taught to pamper myself, but that was exactly what I did. I constantly wanted to take breaks. But this woman made me realize that I had more strength than I gave myself credit for. So I challenged myself and kept up my spirit. When I got tired, one look at these elder role models somehow brightened me and gave me the strength to push myself a little harder.

One day we shot a scene in a muddy rice field over and over again; and the refugees (especially the elders) just smiled and laughed and enjoyed what they were doing. Their attitude was, "That was fun." They made me smile. I joined their laughter and the hours slipped away. Once I turned work into fun, I became energized and could go on for hours without wearing down. These people reminded me of how it was to have fun. As a child, while other children played in the rain, I was forced to stay indoors and watch. So, during a rainy scene I recalled the urge to run in the rain—and this made performing in the muddy rice field fun and easy. I became productive.

Having the refugees there made it easy to think that work was fun. When I was on my own, I frequently used to get depressed, burnt out, and fed up with school. Now I know to remind myself to look at school from a new perspective. There was a time I longed for the education I was deprived of because of lack of money. I wanted to be able to read and educate myself. Yet when I was given the opportunity to get an education in America, I somehow took it for granted. I had forgotten to learn. Now I have become more enthusiastic about studying. I am enjoying all that I do, so opening a book or reading the next chapter is not a difficult thing. There is no hesitation, just anticipation. This is the discipline I gained from observing the behavior of the refugees: for one to continue, one must look at life positively.

One time I asked the refugees if they felt mistreated or overworked. They pointed out that the assistant producers and directors were on their feet the earliest and would still be on their feet after we, the actors, had gone home. They suggested, "Try to be considerate of others' effort. Life is hard on everyone." And they were right. I could get my own food and water; and there was plenty of ground to sit on. Why make someone go out of his way to get a seat I don't need? Why should I complain about being tired when the other crew members continued to work without a word of complaint? It was elementary, yet I needed the refugees to point it out to me.

The way these refugees lived the moral values I grew up with made me realize that morals are important to life. They reinforced many of the values I thought were idealistic. The two stories I love most are about the laws of karma and cause and effect—they reminded me things exist for a purpose.

One story is about the water buffalo. The water buffalo may be big and ugly, but it is obedient, hardworking, and kind. It plows the field without breaks and eats only the unwanted weeds. It is still of use after its death: its meat can be eaten, its fur, horns, and bones can be used as clothes and for shelter and protection. The water buffalo is, in fact, a beautiful and noble animal to my people.

Another story is about the cat and the dog, and teaches the law of karma. The dog may abuse the cat now, but in its next life it must undo the damage and must pay for its wrongdoings. The dog may be in a different form—even reincarnated as a cat!—and may be taken advantage of by the cat that has now been reincarnated into a dog!

Practicing the laws of karma all their lives seems to be what makes these farmers as caring, compassionate, and understanding as they are.

As the refugees put it, if you are content, you can pursue your journey without losing focus. "Be patient in your course because regardless of how long it takes to fulfill your dream, as long as you get there with contentment, the struggles and frustrations can only enhance your satisfaction. If you have patience, your attempts will be effortless. But if you are impatient, everything you do may be such an effort that you no longer want to share what you worked so hard for. Impatience may let you succeed earlier, but will you be free with your success, or will you live in fear and discontent? Wherever you are, be free with yourself—don't stand on an apex but on an open platform where you are free to run, roam and explore." The refugees said and did just that. Their priority was to keep their family together. They were content with where they were and what they were.

It seems everybody starts out with the intention of working to support the family, because building a family gives one joy and happiness. But somehow, along the way, maybe because we try too hard, we begin to lose focus. Instead of building a family, we build a business. Once the family breaks apart, we break, too.

The way the refugees taught me their wisdom was by speaking and sharing with me instead of lecturing. I guess that was what clicked.

Having learned these lessons, I came to understand that like everything else, making a movie is like building a family: it takes team work. I could not have done the job as well as I did without those who had the knowledge and experience to help me. For instance, the feelings of sadness that poured out of Oliver Stone, Le Ly, and the refugees gave me a sense of the destruction and torment caused by war. I am not old enough to remember the war, so I could only read about it. While there was action in front of the camera, I noticed more what was happening behind the camera. The extras broke down like children in the midst of warfare! Seeing the pain and misery that resurfaced from their experiences of war touched me in ways reading and watching TV never did. The refugees related their stories about deaths and family split-ups through tears. Having witnessed the scene behind the camera, I came to understand and empathize with the victims of war. I became more in tune with the feelings of helplessness I had when I lost touch with my family.

Then there was the divorce episode in the film. I had never been married nor had I ever known anyone who got divorced. I could not relate any of my experiences to a divorce. Fortunately, I had Le Ly and Nadia Venesse, the voice coach, to open up and share their feelings of failure and frustration because of their divorces. Through facial expressions they revealed how ugly and evil one becomes during a divorce. They formed fists near their womb when they spoke of the fight over custody of their children. And the way they fluttered and gasped for air while they spoke taught me how emotionally unstable one can become. The pain and emotion was so real. Yet they were willing to let these feelings resurface in my behalf because they wanted me to be as proud as I could be of my performance. Without them, I would be in front of the camera day in and out shooting the same scenes still.

I was among these men and women who seemed so strong and wise, yet were so vulnerable. On the outside, a man like Oliver can appear to be tough and demanding, but inside he is as vulnerable and caring as the rest. People say that strength and wisdom help you to overcome your vulnerability, but, as I recall, these strong and wise people were quite vulnerable. At one point, I went into a state of seclusion due to the emotional trauma of having done the rape scene. I had constant nightmares, I was afraid to look at or speak to anyone because I thought I might bring them into my sleep. So I closed myself in. There was not one person on location who was not concerned. When I refused to let them help, they felt helpless and vulnerable. Yet they did not let my rejection turn them away. They looked for different tactics to get me to open up. They sought professional help and asked those close to me to stay by my side. I knew their concern was genuine. My performance was not affected by my trauma, but they attempted to help me overcome it anyhow. I remember Oliver coming into my trailer to try and speak to me. He was not successful and was hurt like the others. But he did not give up.

I don't know why I had their affection, but I thank every one of them for their concern for my welfare. Their efforts to cheer me up, to comfort me, and to be there for me will always stay with me.

My experiences in this movie are priceless. This interracial family in my microcosmic world reinforced the Asian and American in me. The words and actions of my Vietnamese family deepened my sense of identity. And the will of my American family to help and to care taught me to trust and to lean on family as backbone. The making of the movie is long gone, yet both sides of my family still keep in touch. That is what care and concern is about: not just a business deal, but a relationship. These two parts of my family are fundamental elements of my world. I have always been blessed, but this movie is by far one of the best blessings.

Oliver Stone, seated on a Chapman Crane with cinematographer Bob Richardson, lines up a shot on location in a Simi Valley, California, neighborhood that doubled for the more southerly San Diego.

THE STORY BEHIND THE STORY

by Michael Singer

In the delicate, lyrical Vietnamese language, the word for "rice chaff"—*gao kho*—not only describes the light, dried husk that blows away in the wind, but is also the name that the peasant farmers applied to themselves during decades of war. As their country was turned into an incendiary chessboard by successive waves of players with conflicting ideologies—the French, the Vietnamese of both communist and capitalist persuasions, and, finally, the Americans—the peasants were swept up in great historical gales and twisted in a thousand different directions. North to south, east to west, and back again, they were at the mercy of forces much more powerful than themselves.

It is the unique and unexplored perspective of one of these courageous survivors that attracted Oliver Stone to Le Ly Hayslip's extraordinary tale.

"Le Ly's story is about humanity, growth, and wisdom," says Stone, whose own tribulations as a decorated veteran of the Vietnam War informed his two previous cinematic examinations of the conflict, the award-winning *Platoon* and *Born on the Fourth of July*. But this time the point of view is different and, to American and European audiences, completely new. Until now, the Vietnamese have remained an unexplored abstraction to most people in the West—nameless faces that passed before our eyes on TV news broadcasts, their fate always of secondary concern to our national interests.

Even before the huge, worldwide success of *JFK* confirmed his position as America's most exciting filmmaker, Oliver Stone had decided that Le Ly Hayslip's life story would serve as the foundation for his next film project. It was called to his attention by Robert Kline, a former president of Hayslip's East Meets West organization (later to be one of the producers of *Heaven and Earth*).

"I read Le Ly's first book, *When Heaven and Earth Changed Places*, and it was a great read from beginning to end." Stone recalls. "It was an epic journey, an odyssey, and I fell in love with both the project and Le Ly.

"But for some reason," continues Stone, "I felt that there was an element missing from the story that would help to make it a really great movie."

Stone discovered that missing element while on a Vietnam Airlines flight from Hanoi to Ho Chi Minh City, the former Saigon, during a research trip with Hayslip.

"Le Ly was writing the second book—*Child of War, Woman of Peace*—and the manuscript was on her lap. I asked her what it was, and Le Ly said that it was just something she was writing about her life in America. I grabbed it, started reading it on the airplane, and knew by the end of chapter one that I had found the third act of the film."

If there is one element that links all of Oliver Stone's films, it is his protagonists' odysseys into enlightenment, whether political, spiritual, or both. (Even in *The Doors*, Jim Morrison's excessive quest for the unknowable leads him to a wide-eyed stare in that Paris bathtub, seeing . . . what?)

Stone found himself irrevocably drawn to the most indomitable aspect of Le Ly Hayslip's own odyssey: her unshakable spiritual faith. This was not something Stone was so attuned to when serving as a young infantryman in Vietnam during the 1960s.

"What was interesting about Le Ly's story was its chance for me to step outside of my own experience again," notes Stone, "to see the war from another point of view. The war completely eradicated the infrastructure of the country, the agricultural structure, and made the people dependent on government. That's what militarization seems to come to, government control. So there was a division: people were put into hamlets and removed from their ancient cemeteries where they worshipped their ancestors, which I found out is a key element of their universe.

"Ancestor worship is the core of Buddhism and spirituality in the East. When that was taken, as well as their traditional agricultural support system, the people were never able to get it back. That was one of the great underlying tragedies of Vietnam that I was never aware of as an infantryman."

Stone was determined to preserve that appreciation of Vietnamese spirituality as one of the film's fundamental cores, perhaps the first time it would be so explored in a Western film. He also decided—with Hayslip's blessing—to employ creative license, condensing and broadening her story to create a film with a visual and dramatic life of its own. For example, the character of Sgt. Steve Butler—played by Tommy Lee Jones—is a composite of four American men who had a profound impact on Le Ly's life, both in Vietnam and in the United States. Butler is an emblem of the courage, confusion, and tragic desperation experienced by so many veterans, both during and after the war.

Toting her ever-present straw fan, Le Ly Hayslip gets a hug from actress Hiep Thi Le on location in Thailand. The two women developed a close friendship based on common experience and a mutual desire to properly transfer the emotional reality of Hayslip's life to screen.

The Qui Nhon Highway exodus scene required monumental coordination of more than a thousand people, hundreds of vehicles, even animals. Many crew members climbed atop the equipment trucks, seen on the left, in order to take in the whole breathtaking vista.

The invaders and the invaded of Vietnam developed strong bonds of mutually shared experience that often led them into passionate but troubled relationships. For these people, the war didn't end with the fall of Saigon—a point that both Stone and Hayslip felt was crucial to the film.

As Stone brought his production team together—among them producer A. Kitman Ho, coproducer Clayton Townsend, director of photography Robert Richardson, production designer Victor Kempster, costume designer Ha Nguyen, film editors David Brenner and Sally Menke, assistant Richard Rutowski, and military advisor Dale Dye—casting agents Risa Bramon Garcia, Billy Hopkins, and Heidi Levitt commenced one of the most unusual talent searches in film history. Stone decided that most of the Vietnamese roles in the story—including that of Le Ly herself—would primarily be filled by Asian nonprofessionals, and by Vietnamese nonprofessionals as often as possible.

Rather than consider the casting of nonprofessionals to be a risk, Oliver Stone felt that their contribution to *Heaven and Earth* would be a major one. "First-time people are always underestimated," he emphasizes. "But they come from real life. They haven't been corrupted by the movie process, where often we get more distant from real life because we get more blinders and more people that prevent the truth from getting in. I think that first-time people are the hope of the business in many ways."

Casting got underway in September 1991, with open calls held throughout the United States and Canada, wherever large communities of *Viet Kieu*—former Vietnamese nationals now living elsewhere—were situated. In San Francisco; Santa Fe; Houston; Dallas; New Orleans; Virginia; Washington, DC; Orange County in California; Vancouver—sixteen thousand Vietnamese responded to advertisements in newspapers and on television.

Casually responding to one of the open calls in Northern California—"because all my friends were doing it for fun"—was Hiep Thi Le, a young physiology major attending the University of California at Davis. Born in Da Nang, Central Vietnam—very near to Le Ly's home village of Ky La—Hiep exited her country in 1979 as a nine-year-old "boat person," undergoing a dangerous journey with a

Director of photography Bob Richardson operates the camera during a dramatic encounter between Le Ly (Hiep Thi Le) and Mama (Joan Chen). Director Stone, watching his video monitors, reacts enthusiastically to the actresses' performances.

Debbie Reynolds, one of the entertainment world's true legends, had not made a feature film for twenty years until Oliver Stone lured her back to the screen for the role of Eugenia, the mother of Sergeant Steve Butler (Tommy Lee Jones).

on their own quest for emotional and dramatic reality by visiting the real Ky La in Central Vietnam. There, Hayslip and her mother—still active at eighty-five—taught Stone and the actors about life in a traditional farming village.

"The goal of this trip was twofold," says Stone. "One was for me to renew my acquaintance with Vietnamese farming and village life, the sense, smell, and feel of the countryside. The other was to introduce Hiep and Joan to the rigors of farm life. I wanted them to get up early, sleep in the house, dig, hoe, walk barefoot in the paddies. It was hard for both women, but crucial to the reality they had to bring to their roles."

Joan Chen took advantage of the trip to speak with many Vietnamese women who had much in common, culturally and experientially, with her character of Mama Phung. "I looked into these women's eyes and listened to what they had gone through: the war, the poverty, the strength, and the pride. Their eyes were completely without ego. They were just there, like a tree growing."

Visiting Ky La marked Hiep Thi Le's first return to Vietnam since leaving thirteen years before, and it led to a joyous reunion with relatives who last knew her as a little girl. "When I was chosen to play Le Ly, it was beyond my expectations," she told a Vietnamese reporter. "The day when Oliver Stone told me I would be returning to the country where I was born, all I could do was cry and cry. I am still awestruck. I can't believe that I'm back home among relatives I've loved and missed for so long."

Also joining Stone and company on their Vietnam odyssey was Kitaro, the hugely popular Japanese-born recording and performing artist, chosen by the director to write the music score for *Heaven and Earth* . . . thus marking the composer's first foray into an English-language film.

Kitaro practices both Buddhism and the traditional Japanese religion of Shinto, and his music has always reflected a deep sensitivity to nature, humanity, and spirituality, three of the most important elements contained within the film.

Another extraordinary journey would also take place in Vietnam: director of photography Robert Richardson and a camera assistant, along with Victor Kempster and Le Ly Hayslip, spent two tough but fruitful weeks traveling throughout the country with a 35-millimeter Panavision camera and twenty-six pieces of equipment. Their mission: to film establishing shots of landscapes, cityscapes, and people that would ultimately be seamlessly woven into the body of the final movie to lend even greater authenticity to *Heaven and Earth*.

"My experiences shooting second unit in Vietnam were some of the greatest pleasures I had on this film," recalls Richardson. "The country is remarkable for its physical diversity and the spirit of its people. I was often overwhelmed by contrasting feelings of guilt and rage. My country, the United States, unleashed such a barrage of destruction and carnage during the war that I was surprised to see such a flowering could take place. We were given complete freedom of movement, and this total cooperation resulted in some of the most stunning images of the film."

The camera crew films Tommy Lee Jones and Dale Dye in their roles as Sergeant Steve Butler and his marine comrade Larry, making a rushed and dangerous landing at An Khe during a Viet Cong attack to rescue Le Ly and the children.

With the construction of Ky La finally completed in Phang-Nga (although delayed by a few weeks because of destruction to the rice fields by a late monsoon), principal photography began on October 19, 1992, following several days of shooting detailed, documentary-like scenes of village life.

Then the action really started.

"There are two kinds of movies you can work on," says coproducer Clayton Townsend. "Oliver's . . . and everybody else's. It's just

130

One of America's most versatile actors, Tommy Lee Jones had previously co-starred for Oliver Stone as the sinister Clay Shaw in JFK, *which brought him an Oscar nomination. Jones was attracted to* Heaven and Earth *not only by the power of Le Ly Hayslip's life story, but also by Stone's screenplay, which Jones called "an epic poem."*

downright amazing. Oliver is unique in working at the pace that he does. I've never seen anybody work with that kind of fervor."

Anyone working on *Heaven and Earth* would confirm that there was at least three times as much activity at any given moment than on other film sets. *Heaven and Earth* was often an astonishing six-ring circus of thunderous movement and forward momentum. While Stone would be shooting an important scene featuring much dialogue and action, about half a mile away—in the rice paddies at the foothills of the limestone peaks overhanging Ky La—retired Marine captain Dale Dye, the film's military adviser, might be using his God-given hell-

Sitting inside "her" house—an exact recreation of the home in Ky La still lived in by her mother—Le Ly Hayslip receives a cooling sweep of the fan from Joan Chen during the break in the shooting of a traditional feast sequence.

Early morning in the pastoral beauty of production designer Victor Kempster's re-created village of Ky La, with the cool mist hugging the surrounding limestone peaks.

hath-no-fury talents to whip a bunch of extras into shape as a platoon of American GIs.

A mile or two beyond, Mike Stokey—another military adviser who, like Stone and Dye, had served his country in Vietnam—might be applying his knowledge of fighting the Viet Cong to create a core group of VC for the movie from a diverse assortment that included Chinese and Vietnamese youths from Hong Kong and Thailand, not to mention a woman college student from San Francisco.

Perhaps second unit director Philip Pfeiffer would be at the other end of the village, shooting detailed scenes of rice harvesting, or a traditional Vietnamese opera company in performance.

Meanwhile, the Thai army might be rolling tanks and armored vehicles—each repainted with the markings of the US Army—down the one road that connected Ky La with the main Phuket/Phang-Nga highway.

All in a day's work, and there were sixty-four of them, each one a veritable maelstrom of creativity.

By any cinematic standards, *Heaven and Earth* was a grand-scale, even monumental production. The entire cast and crew—which numbered more than a thousand people during the Thailand portion of the shoot—was composed of a bewildering mélange of nationalities, including American, Thai, Vietnamese, British, Australian, Cambodian, Laotian, Hong Kong Chinese, Malaysian Chinese, Mainland Chinese and French, among others. Miraculously, communication problems were at a minimum, since film is something of an international language.

On a given day—for example, Tuesday, November 3, 1992, the thirteenth day of principal photography—the call sheet indicated the need for 22 principal actors, 1,500 extras, 50 ARVN (South Vietnamese) soldier extras, 9 prison guard extras, and 6 reporter extras, plus two dozen bicycles, two news vans, eight ox carts, three dozen old vehicles (including buses), machine-gun turrets, sandbags, ten boats, and a helicopter. In just one shooting day, Stone would film not only Le Ly's release from My Thi Prison, but also the mammoth Qui Nhon highway sequence.

If there was a beating heart at the locus of the production, it was the village. And for the *Viet Kieu* actors, seeing Ky La for the first time was a deeply emotional experience.

"When I saw Ky La, I started crying," recalls US government worker Lan Nguyen Calderon, who plays Le Ly's sister, Ba. "The roads were so much like those when I went to visit my aunt in Da Nang. The village, the smells, the sights were so real."

"We all burst into tears," agrees San Francisco State University teacher Mai Le Ho, who portrays the sister Hai. "We all thought, my God, how I miss home. Most of us live pretty mainstream lives in America, and we're so busy being productive members of society that we forget what it means to be Vietnamese. We forget what our homeland is like. Ky La reminded us."

The Ky La of *Heaven and Earth* was populated not only by the actors and nonprofessionals cast by Stone, but also by two hundred "core villagers," extras recruited by Hong Kong-based casting agent Pat Pao from northeastern Thailand, where thousands of Vietnamese refugees—many of them born in Thailand—still live in camps.

For these people, contributing to the texture of *Heaven and Earth* was at first a wary challenge, but finally a profound labor of love. "They were concerned about working on a movie by Americans," notes Le Ly Hayslip, "because a lot of these people were from the North. They told me, 'The Americans burned our land . . . why should we help them?' But when they learned that people from all over the world had come to tell their story, they were anxious to participate."

Adds Pat Pao: "Working on *Heaven and Earth* was an opportunity for these people to really express their pride in being Vietnamese, a chance to get back and work the land again like they did in their own country. They all came to love and adore both Le Ly and Hiep, treating them like lost sisters, mothers, and daughters. This pride is something that a lot of them have been suppressing for the last thirty years."

The "core villagers" were eager to share that pride with their new American friends. One wizened old man recited:

All my life I will forever miss

> *My country*

> *My home*

> *My land*

> *It doesn't matter where I am*

> *Am I for Vietnam?*

> *Am I for my homeland?*

> *Yes!*

Another man born in Central Vietnam—in fact, in the next village over from Ky La—spoke movingly of his emotions: "We are so

In synchronized concentration, Oliver Stone and Hiep Thi Le work out a scene outside of Ky La's temple.

135

One of the world's great beauties, Joan Chen willingly and happily eschewed glamor for realism as Le Ly's indomitable mother, even to her betel-stained teeth and complex aging makeup for the latter part of the film.

happy to see this movie being made. People working here from all over the world are using their hearts, minds, bodies, and physical strength, day and night, to tell our story. This is a movie for the whole world to see and understand. We are refugees from the wars. We take refuge in all parts of the world. We are in Thailand. Some of our new friends are in America. We are everywhere except our home . . . Vietnam."

This man had been absent from Vietnam for the last forty-seven of his seventy years. And the closest he had come to returning was in this reconstructed village of Ky La, on Petkasem Road, Amphur Muang, Phang-Nga district, Thailand.

The Vietnamese and *Viet Kieu* cast and extras especially enjoyed wearing the traditional comfortable Vietnamese peasant clothing, mostly of black, brown, or maroon cotton weave. Costume designer Ha Nguyen—herself a native of Hue, the imperial city in Central Vietnam—had more than 90 percent of the costumes "built" within

As Le Ly's strong and sensitive father, Dr. Haing Ngor carried to his role a lifetime of suffering and triumph. Having survived the horrific Khmer Rouge regime in his native Cambodia, Dr. Ngor has dedicated his life to helping and teaching, whether through direct action or what he calls "films with a purpose . . . like Heaven and Earth.

137

eight weeks by hand. One thousand yards of cotton produced about twenty-five hundred pieces of clothing, which were dyed and then aged. The *non la*—that functional, yet beautiful lampshade-shaped farmer's hat of Vietnam—was brought in by the hundreds. Nguyen would also design the lovely *ao dais* that Hiep Thi Le wore in certain scenes; the traditional garment is perhaps one of the world's most flattering to the female figure.

The movie village of Ky La became a second home for much of the cast and crew of *Heaven and Earth*, and not only because most of their days (and many of their nights) were spent there working. Le Ly Hayslip enjoyed several nights sleeping in "her" house—an exact re-creation of the home her mother still lives in, cooking dinner and tending the chickens, pigs, and ducks. For those born in Vietnam, it was like going home. For the *Viet Kieu* either born elsewhere or with little memory of their country, it was an experience that linked them with a dimly perceived heritage.

Dustin Nguyen, who portrays Le Ly's beloved older brother, Sau, has heretofore been the most famous *Viet Kieu* actor in America, partially due to his role as Harry Ioki on the popular TV series "21 Jump Street." But his experiences on *Heaven and Earth* led Nguyen into some unexpected places of the heart.

"For me," says Nguyen, "being in Ky La with other Vietnamese actors, all in costume, was like being transported to a place where I felt at home, even though it was a movie set. My heart felt for the first time that it belonged to Vietnam, which I hadn't been in touch with in the eighteen years that have passed since I left there.

"I had lost a lot of my roots through the inevitable process of Americanization," Nguyen adds, "but spending day in and day out in Ky La brought me face-to-face with the world of my ancestors."

The four-walled, solid-roofed buildings of Ky La served practical purposes as well, functioning as storage facilities for the unit's voluminous equipment and as between-takes shelter for the actors. One "house" was special: as the sole air-conditioned structure in the entire village, it was the base of operations for Academy Award-winning (*Bram Stoker's Dracula*) make-up artist Matthew Mungle and hair stylist Elle Elliott and their staffs. In the fiery heat and humidity, Mungle and Elliott required cool conditions in which to apply their often elaborate and technically sensitive creations, particularly for the "aging" prosthetics of certain actors whose characters gain nearly forty years in the course of the story.

The village's radiant little Buddhist temple, a brisk walk across the rice paddies, became an authentic place of worship and meditation for many Asian cast and crew members (as well as for the local villagers working in Ky La), and a quiet refuge for Westerners seeking a peaceful respite. Indeed, many of the Americans and Europeans working on *Heaven and Earth* not only picked up several phrases of Thai and Vietnamese, but bits and pieces of Buddhism as well. More than one returned home with a neck draped with traditional Thai Buddhist amulets to bring good karma and ward off bad luck.

If the village had any imperfections, it was that it was just too perfect! Ky La was constructed for realism, not comfort, and moving the heavy equipment across bumpy dirt roads and rice paddies provided several uproarious and exhausting moments for the crew. Virtually everyone, at one time or another, slipped off the burms and into the

Oliver Stone directs Hiep Thi Le and Dr. Haing Ngor in Le Ly and Papa's emtional farewell scene on the temple wall. Few crew members were left dry-eyed during the filming of this sequence.

139

Le Ly Hayslip relived a lifetime during the sixty-four days of filming Heaven and Earth, *often requiring solitude to collect her thoughts and memories. For this, Hayslip would take comfort sitting in or near "her" house, a re-creation of her actual home in Ky La.*

muddy murk of the paddies. One of the victims was Oliver Stone's video assistant, Marty Kassab, who took the dive with a cart full of TV monitors . . . and a playful push from cinematographer Bob Richardson.

In the story, Ky La is devastated by the effects of war and the presence of an American military base, and for the purposes of the film, the *Heaven and Earth* art department—which so lovingly crafted the village into its pristine condition—now faced the awful task of destroying it.

"It's not the kind of thing you really want to do," observes Victor Kempster, "but of course, we had to. It was all in service of the story. We tried to save as much rice as we could when we burnt the paddies, and then we beat the buildings to hell—blew up some, torched others."

Hiep Thi Le witnessed the emotional responses to the destruction of Ky La by several of the core villagers. One of these Vietnamese refugees—perhaps dealing with his own painful memories of war—burst into tears as he watched a house go up in flames. No one involved with *Heaven and Earth* remained unmoved. For some, it was like watching a piece of their life being wrenched away.

"I was one of the last people to see the village after we finished working there," recalls Clayton Townsend. "It had been stripped of all set dressing, either by us or the villagers. What was left were the husks of bent-over rice, remainders of the temple and the shells of the buildings. It was sad because of the kinship that we all had encountered as a filming unit. It also made me think of what it must have been like for Le Ly to have returned home to see such devastation for real."

Oliver Stone, who often stayed in Ky La overnight, remembered "waking up at five in the morning with a pink light coming down from the mountains. It was a beautiful little village, a bit like Brigadoon, in a way. It will have a special place in my heart forever."

When "wrap" was called in the village for the last time by first assistant director Herb Gains, there was a small celebration among the cast and crew, with toasts over beer and champagne. The core villagers hurried with their Instamatics to have their pictures taken with Oliver Stone, Hiep Thi Le, and Le Ly Hayslip, proudly posing with their new friends.

In a private moment, an American crew member stepped to the side of a ruined village building, clasped his hands together in the traditional Asian devotional manner, and bowed to the four directions—

A tracking shot of the Republican colonel, portrayed by Peter Duong, addressing the villagers on the set of Ky La.

thanking whatever spirits and ancestors had watched over the company throughout the long weeks of filming in the valley that gave a home to Ky La.

But Thailand also provided myriad other locations for *Heaven and Earth,* particularly the urban landscapes of Phuket Town and Bangkok, in which Victor Kempster and his staff re-created large hunks of period Da Nang and Saigon.

Phuket Town's picturesque Sino-Portuguese shophouses served Stone and Kempster's purposes perfectly, with Vietnamese signage completing the illusion. A magnificent "Penang"-style mansion, built by a wealthy Chinese merchant in 1915, served as the location for the aristocratic Anh and Madame Lien's residence. The art department enhanced the humidity-drenched, atmospheric decadence of the house with solid old European furniture, and set decorators even had hundreds of vintage Vietnamese books flown in from Saigon for the house's library.

So authentic were some of the re-creations of Da Nang in Phuket Town that Le Ly Hayslip, riding through the small city with her son Alan one Sunday morning, licked her chops at the sight of a sign in Vietnamese announcing that *pho*—her country's ever-popular noodle-and-beef soup—was served at that particular establishment. Unfortunately, her excitement was quashed when she discovered that the sign was merely the work of a scenic artist for a segment of the movie to be shot two days later.

142

Filming in Bangkok required fifteen locations in six days, a brutal schedule in one of the most congested, polluted megacities on the planet.

"I would say that the most challenging element of filming in Bangkok was Bangkok itself," muses Victor Kempster. "I mean, getting from one side of town to the other could take six hours. And crossing the street was a liability to your health."

Much of the Bangkok filming occurred in the city's bustling Chinatown district, one of the oldest quarters of the metropolis. Filled with evocative alleyways and pungent storefronts, Chinatown provided its own curious obstacles, as Clayton Townsend discovered.

"We had trouble putting up our Vietnamese signs because shopkeepers believed it's bad luck to take down their own!" he recounts. "There's no way around it; they won't change. We wound up having to find other ways to block off the Chinese- and Thai-language signs."

But the *pièce de résistance* occurred on the very last day of shooting in Bangkok. For the purposes of a huge scene shot in the Royal Plaza, tanks, armored cars, and other military vehicles were

Papa (Dr. Haing Ngor) tearfully walks away from the burning embers of the first Phung family home, torched by the French during their 1953 incursion into Ky La. This was a moment that Le Ly Hayslip found difficult to watch, still remembering the humble straw-and-thatch house in which she was born.

Hundreds of hectares of fallow rice fields in Phang-Nga were replanted and painstakingly tended to create the verdant and nurturing beauty that surrounds Ky La.

brought in by the production, along with thousands of extras, many of them in military uniform.

Thailand had suffered a major military coup just a couple of months before *Heaven and Earth* began filming, and rumor soon spread throughout the city that another one was under way: The palace and government buildings were under siege! The next day, newspapers and TV broadcasts had to quiet the fears of the nation. After all, it was only a movie.

After breaking for the Christmas and New Year holidays, the *Heaven and Earth* company—or what remained after its Thai friends and colleagues remained behind—regrouped in Los Angeles for the American portion of the shoot in early January of 1993. Everyone missed Thailand and its paradisiacal charms, but the crew looked forward to easier working conditions and Southern California's typically seasonable weather conditions.

No such luck.

The four weeks of shooting in Los Angeles were infused with buckets of rain and cutting wind.

"In some ways," sighed Clayton Townsend at the time, "Thailand was easier."

For Oliver Stone, Bob Richardson, and Victor Kempster, the American section of the story represented a unique opportunity to view the country through the eyes of an ever-astonished recent arrival, Le Ly. They decided upon a visual style of slightly heightened realism, as if the audience is allowed to walk in Le Ly's not-yet-broken-in American shoes. "It was charmed up somewhat to suggest the impact that America would have on someone who was totally alien to the place," notes Clayton Townsend. "After all, the greens of a jungle are a lot brighter to someone from New York City than to someone who was born there."

"Stylistically, our scenes in Vietnam and Thailand descended from natural beauty and spiritual purity," says Bob Richardson. "The

Joan Chen, Dr. Haing Ngor and their "kids" take a lunch break in the rice paddies. On the extreme right is Thuan Nguyen, an engineer now living in Texas, who, as an ARVN officer during the war, was imprisoned by the Viet Cong for seven years. Selected by Oliver Stone to portray Uncle Luc, Nguyen saw the film as a great opportunity to help heal the rifts between Vietnamese of different political persuasions.

145

United States was only one step in the process of understanding the spiritual journey of Le Ly. The style of shooting was not bound to a visual metaphor that can be immediately defined or confined to one country or another. Beauty and ugliness, spirituality and physicality can be found in balance."

Nearing the end of filming, the company attempted to put the entire epic experience into some kind of perspective. "I'm still in shock," Le Ly Hayslip admitted at the time. "I haven't really been able to sit down and review it all from beginning to end. I actually feel sort of guilty that so many people had to work so hard to tell my story. When the weather is so bad and the conditions are terrible, I feel like a troublemaker. But it's been so much positive energy for everybody to pull together and make this movie. There seems to be a feeling of mission from Oliver and everyone on the crew.

"Most people relive their life the moment before they die," she observes. "I've relived it in the middle of my life. But every morning I see the faces of these people whom I have come to love, and now we're all going on to different directions. We came together for a brief time to make something special come to life. It's as if my family is breaking up all over again."

But Le Ly Hayslip has a strongly held dream for what *Heaven and Earth* may accomplish with audiences around the world: "to open up people's hearts and minds . . . to allow them to accept their fellow human beings as brothers and sisters . . . to give people a chance to live their own destiny . . . to make them understand that war is never the answer."

Oliver Stone has similar hopes: "We are heading toward a new era in the twenty-first century, I hope, of total consciousness. People of all color will be sharing this planet. It's necessary for us to get out of our skins and cross this spiritual and divisive gulf that people have formed.

"*Heaven and Earth* is the story of one Vietnamese woman and her family that's played out again and again wherever strife replaces love. Therefore, it's a universal tale, accessible to everyone, everywhere. Hopefully, a Vietnamese woman will matter to an African in the Sudan or an Indian in Bombay or an American in Tuscaloosa. There are no borders between human experience. Suffering occurs everywhere . . . and thank God, so can enlightenment."

The village's temple, at the foot of the limestone peaks overhanging Ky La, became a place of quiet refuge for many in the company, Buddhist and otherwise. Although built as a movie set, it was quickly seen as a real place of worship and contemplation . . . a pleasant surprise to its creator, production designer Victor Kempster.

FILM CREDITS

WARNER BROS. Presents

In Association with

REGENCY ENTERPRISES, LE STUDIO CANAL +,

and ALCOR FILMS

An IXTLAN/MILCHAN/TRANS-ATLANTIC ENTERPRISES Production

An OLIVER STONE Film

"Heaven and Earth"

TOMMY LEE JONES

JOAN CHEN

HAING S. NGOR

and introducing HIEP THI LE

Edited by DAVID BRENNER, SALLY MENKE

Production Designer VICTOR KEMPSTER

Director of Photography ROBERT RICHARDSON, A.S.C.

Music Composed by KITARO

Co-Producer CLAYTON TOWNSEND

Executive Producer MARIO KASSAR

Produced by

OLIVER STONE, ARNON MILCHAN, ROBERT KLINE, A. KITMAN HO

Screenplay by OLIVER STONE
Based upon the books *When Heaven and Earth Changed Places*, by LE LY
HAYSLIP with JAY WURTS, and *Child of War, Woman of Peace*,
by LE LY HAYSLIP with JAMES HAYSLIP

Directed by OLIVER STONE

PHOTOGRAPHY CREDITS

ROLAND NEVEU is a French-born, Bangkok-based photographer. A noted photojournalist, Neveu also served as unit photographer on Oliver Stone's *Platoon, Born on the Fourth of July*, and the Thailand section of *Heaven and Earth*. His photography appears on pages 1, 2, 8-9, 10, 12, 14, 15, 16, 17, 18, 19, 20, 22, 23, 24, 25, 26, 27, 28, 29, 30, 31, 32, 33, 34, 35, 36, 37, 38, 39, 40, 41, 42, 43, 44, 45, 46, 47, 48, 49, 51, 52, 54, 55, 58, 59, 61, 65, 66, 67, 68, 69, 92, 94, 95, 97, 98, 99, 100, 103 105, 112, 121, 122, 123, 131, 132, 135, 136, 137, 141, 142, 143, 144, 147.

SIDNEY BALDWIN is a photographer who has worked with Oliver Stone on *The Doors, JFK*, the United States section of *Heaven and Earth*, and the forthcoming *Natural Born Killers*, also by Oliver Stone. His photography appears on pages 70, 71, 72, 73, 74, 75, 78, 79, 80, 82, 83, 84, 85, 87, 89, 90, 91, 118, 128.

ELIZABETH STONE hails from Texas. Her first camera was given to her by Oliver Stone in 1979, the year of his first film. She's been documenting his films ever since, and has done photography for *Platoon, Born on the Fourth of July, The Doors, JFK,* and *Heaven and Earth*. Her photography has been published widely in magazines on the film industry, and appears here on pages 53, 57, 106, 124, 127, 130, 139, 145.

EAST MEETS WEST
FOUNDATION

A Humanitarian Relief and Development Organization

Le Ly Hayslip made a visit to her homeland of Viet Nam in 1986 for the first time since leaving fifteen years earlier. Her homecoming was both enlightening and disheartening as she witnessed the pain and poverty that the Vietnamese people endure every day. Upon her return, she established an organization whose purpose is to identify and respond effectively to the many needs of Viet Nam's people.

1989   *Built Mother's Love Health Clinic in Ky La, Viet Nam*

1990   *Shipped 10 tons of medical supplies to Viet Nam*

1991   *Opened the Peace Village Medical Clinic, where 100 patients receive free medical exams and medicine daily*

1992   *Initiated Mobile Medical Unit serving 200–500 patients each week in outlying villages*

1992   *Established the Compassion School for children in grades 2 to 5*

1993   *Opened the Displaced Children's Home for 100 children ages 5 to 15 who lack stable care or shelter*

The East Meets West Foundation's mission is to improve the health and socio-economic well-being of Vietnamese families and to provide educational opportunities for the children of Viet Nam.

We are presently seeking funds in order to maintain and expand upon these programs. We appreciate and rely upon the generosity and good will of caring individuals everywhere.

EAST MEETS **WEST**

FOUNDATION
EAST MEETS WEST FOUNDATION
725 Washington Street
Oakland, CA 94607
(510) 834-0301